What Can You Do with a Major in

ENGLISH?

Real people.

Real jobs.

Real rewards.

Shelley O'Hara

Jennifer A. Horowitz,
Series Creator

WILEY

Wiley Publishing, Inc.

For general information on our other products and services or to obtain technical support please contact our Customer Care Department within the U.S. at (800) 762-2974, outside the U.S. at (317) 572-3993 or fax (317) 572-4002.

Wiley also publishes its books in a variety of electronic formats. Some content that appears in print may not be available in electronic books. For more information about Wiley products, please visit our web site at www.wiley.com.

ISBN: 0-7645-7605-4

Library of Congress Cataloging-in-Publication data is available from the publisher upon request.

10 9 8 7 6 5 4 3 2 1

Book design by LeAndra Hosier
Cover design by Sandy St. Jacques
Book production by Wiley Publishing, Inc. Composition Services

Table of Contents

To all of the students in my English W131 classes from the Fall of 2004,
for your enthusiasm, talent, and willingness to see that writing can be fun.
You are the best!

Acknowledgments

Special thanks to Steve Fox, associate professor of English and Associate Chair of the English Department at IUPUI, for spending time answering questions and providing advice based on years of experience teaching English and helping English majors chart a career path. Greg Tubach, thanks for arranging the project; Cindy Kitchel, thanks for recommending me; and Tere Stouffer Drenth, thanks for helping me sharpen and fine-tune the text with your edits and brilliant suggestions.

About This Book

When you make the decision to go to college, the first question people are likely to ask you is, "What are you going to major in?" If you tell them "English," they're likely to think that you want to teach or write, but teaching and writing aren't the only career paths available. In fact, you may not know what careers are relevant to an English degree or what career you want to pursue. And that's fine. That's the purpose of this book: to tell you what types of careers are possible, as well as the advantages and disadvantages of a liberal arts major, such as English.

What Do You Want to Be When You Grow Up?

As a child, you were probably allowed to experiment—play even—with different career ideas. Did you have a little medical kit when you were a child? Did you build architectural marvels with LEGOs? Did you use your chalkboard to teach the other neighborhood kids how to spell properly? Did you have fun playing at whatever career was your fancy that day, week, year, hour?

Even then, though, there was probably some pressure. The medical-kit parents were probably secretly thrilled and may have *casually* mentioned to neighbors and family members, "My child wants to be a doctor!" Although par ents may hav e worried about y our safety, they also probably found common kid car eer choices such as fir efighter or police officer admirable. They probably liked the idea of you're becoming an *astronaut!* But what if y ou wanted to driv e a dump tr uck? or dreamed of being a bartender? Don't parents start to nudge (even push) children toward the careers *they* find acceptable?

And the pr essure doesn't stop ther e. The decision of "what are you going to do with life" escalates as you enter your last few years of high school. By the time you're ready to start college, you may be in an out-and-out panic about choosing a major. And after you finally decide on a major, the advice, judgment, criticism, and suggestions can be ev en more critical and intense. "You're majoring in philosophy? What kind of job can y ou get with a degr ee in philosophy?" O r "An E nglish degree? Who hires people with an English degree in this day and age?"

As the economy has changed, college tuition and r elated costs have increased so dramatically that most students depend on varying degrees of student loans and financial aid, in addition to the sacrifices their families may hav e made to send them to school.　These expenses increase the pressure on you to choose a major based on its marketability, not just on your personal areas of interest. You know that you may be stuck paying back loans for y ears after graduation, so y ou may feel obligated to major in something that will lead to a job that can pay the bills. More pressure!

How This Book Helps You Make Smart Decisions

This book star ts with this message: R elax! S ure, some students kno w right away what they want to study and what they want to do, but the vast majority admit they don 't kno w—or claim they do but secr etly don't. That's okay. Take your time and really think about what major is best for you—that's the first main focus of this book.

It's a myth that a major equals a car eer. Your major prepares you for a career, but not just for one car eer. Your major provides you with lots of varied and different career options. That's the second major purpose of this book. to show you the variety of traditional and nontraditional careers you can pursue in English.

Finally, the job mar ket has changed and continues to change, but there isn't one magic major that will assur e success. B ut you can learn how to make the most of y our major and how to master skills that ar e applicable and transferable to many different fields—making you more marketable. This book also focuses on helping y ou use y our major toward a job that is financially and personally rewarding.

Who This Book Can Help

This book isn 't just for students about to enter college (or about to graduate). Many different people can benefit from the information and skills in this book, including:

◆ High school students who ar e star ting college and ar e unsur e what they want to study

◆ College freshmen or sophomores who are trying to choose a major

◆ College students who are interested in an English major but don't know what career possibilities exist

◆ College students who hav e chosen a major and found that it doesn't suit them (personally , academically, or for whatev er rea- son) and are considering switching to a new major

◆ College students who have already chosen a major in English but are wondering what they might do with this major

◆ College students who ar e E nglish majors but ar e having doubts and are thinking of making a change

◆ Returning students who want to explor e the possibilities of an English major (as a new field of study or as a returning student to English)

◆ People in the workplace who are thinking about switching careers and ar e tr ying to figur e out ho w their E nglish degr ees can help them in that endeavor

A Guide to the Book

The following sections describe some of the featur es you will find in this book. The book star ts with a discussion of majors, colleges, and additional education, and then wor ks its way to car eers, but you don't have to read the book from start to finish. Feel free to read the chapters in whatever order is most helpful to you and your personal situation.

CHAPTER 1: MAJORING IN ENGLISH

If you have already decided on English or are leaning toward this major, read this chapter. You'll discover the basic r equirements for this major and the types of courses you can expect to take, as well as general information and advice about this major.

CHAPTER 2: CHOOSING A COLLEGE

If you're already in college, you don't need help choosing which one to attend. If you haven't decided on a college, though, this chapter can help you determine the key factors to consider in general as well as criteria in particular for English majors.

CHAPTER 3: MAKING THE MOST OF YOUR TIME AT COLLEGE

This chapter provides advice on how to make the most of y our college career (beyond dating and parties!). Instead, you'll find that small steps you take throughout your college years (talking with professors, finding a mentor, joining clubs) can make a big impact later when y   ou ar e about to enter the job market.

CHAPTER 4: ATTENDING GRADUATE SCHOOL IN ENGLISH

Some English majors go on to get a doctorate or master's degree, which can help for some car eer choices (such as teaching at the univ ersity level). You may also get a degr ee in E nglish as a springboar d to law school. In addition to pr oviding advice on ho w to select, get accepted to, and make the most of graduate school, the chapter includes advice for returning students coming back to get adv   anced degrees sev eral years after receiving their undergraduate degree.

CHAPTER 5: BREAKING INTO THE JOB MARKET WITH AN ENGLISH DEGREE

This chapter contains some basic advice on transitioning fr om college life to the working world. It includes tips for finding and applying for jobs, beyond the basic want-ad appr oach. You'll find out ho w to net-work and use the Internet for job advice and hunting, as well use career resources thr ough y our college (including alumni).   This chapter also provides help on preparing for the interview process.

CHAPTER 6: CAREER POSSIBILITIES FOR AN ENGLISH MAJOR

This is a key chapter of this book and describes both the traditional and nontraditional careers y ou can expect to get with a degr ee in E nglish. The chapter gives a summary of the different types of careers, as well as salary and wor k environment information. The chapter also describes any r equired training, go vernment licensing, and other r   egulatory requirements for various careers.

CHAPTER 7: CASE STUDIES

In this chapter, y ou read about sev eral people who graduated with an English major and who hav e used it to go into a v ariety of careers and achieve success. You may be surprised at some of the jobs these people found, as well as how the oppor tunities presented themselves. In these case studies, the par ticipants describe their jobs and explain what they like and dislike about their wor k. They also tell y ou ho w they got to where they ar e today and discuss their successes and mistakes, so that you can benefit from their experiences.

RESOURCE APPENDIX

In the appendix, y ou find a w ealth of other information r elated to an English major and jobs, including:

◆ Honor societies, with contact information

◆ Web sites that offer relevant information

◆ Off-campus career-counseling services

◆ Self-administered aptitude tests and where to find them

◆ Books for further reading

After reading this book, I hope y ou find many ways to make a living from a major in E nglish—one that engages, challenges, and r ewards you personally and financially!

Chapter 1

Majoring in English

An English major, it goes without saying, loves to read and write, and these skills (reading critically and writing effectively) help prepare the student for a variety of different careers, including research, writing, advertising, public relations, journalism, teaching, and more. English is also a good major if you plan to pursue professional schools, such as law, medicine, business, or library science. In the past, an English major may have focused only on British and American writing, but colleges today provide more diverse and flexible coursework, making English a more complex field than many realize. Areas of specialization still include literature, but also include rhetoric and professional communication, creative writing, linguistics, English education, technical communication, and others.

This chapter starts by looking at some general criteria to consider when choosing a major, so that you can make sure English is a good fit for your skills, abilities, and interests. The chapter then covers what to expect if you do decide on a major in English. What courses will you take? What options will you have in selecting classes? What skills will you learn? Finally, this chapter explores the job outlook for English majors.

Choosing a Major

You know what you like, what you're good at, and what inter ests you. Although you may need to do some soul-sear ching and even seek out-side advice, keep in mind that you are in the best position to make the decision of which major is best for you. To help you make this decision, consider what issues are important to you, what resources can provide additional information, and what pitfalls to avoid. Let's start by debunking some myths about picking a major.

THE MYTHS OF CHOOSING A MAJOR

Look at the following statements and see how many you agree with:

◆ Everyone but you knows exactly what major—and car eer—they want.

◆ Your major determines (and limits) your career choices.

◆ You'll just "know" (via a magical sign, omen, or dream) what your major should be.

◆ You should consider the advice of ev eryone when deciding on a major.

◆ You are limited to "one" major.

All of the preceding statements aren't true:

◆ Most students don't know what they want to major in; they strug-gle with this decision as much as you do. According to *U.S. News & World Report's* 2005 college guide, between 20 and 50 percent of students ar e undecided, and about that same per centage will change majors sometime during their college car eers. Even when they have declared a major, students may be unsure about their choice.

◆ Your major and your career are not the same thing. E nglish, like other liberal ar ts majors, pr ovides for a br oad base of skills and experiences, and you can use this major as the opening into any number of fields. Just take a look at the follo wing list of famous people, all with a v ariety of occupations and all with majors in English:

Celebrity	Career
Dave Barry	Columnist for *Miama Herald* and author of several best-selling books
Chevy Chase	Actor
Mario Cuomo	Former Governor of New York
David Duchovny	Actor
Michael Eisner	Walt Disney CEO
Jodie Foster	Actress
Cathy Guisewite	Cartoonist *(Cathy)*
Chris Issak	Singer, songwriter
Stephen Kin	Author
Paul Newman	Actor
Joe Paterno	College football coach
Sally Ride	Astronaut
Diane Sawyer	Broadcast journalist
Marty Shottenheimer	Professional football coach
Paul Simon	Songwriter, singer
Steven Spielberg	Filmmaker
Clarence Thomas	U.S. Supreme Court Justice
Barbara Walters	Broadcast journalist

* cited from www.winthrop.edu

◆ Although it's okay to solicit the help of others, ev eryone has an opinion, but only *you* know what's best for you.

◆ You aren't limited to one area of study. Often, students have multiple interests, and colleges offer many ways to incorporate y our interest into other fields, the most common being minoring in another subject, choosing to get a double-major, or even creating your own specialized major (this is not offered at every school).

◆ As for waiting for the magic sign, it's better to take practical steps (covered in the follo wing section). I f y ou find y ourself in the wrong major, you can switch majors. K eep in mind that the far-ther y ou ar e along in y our college course work and the type of major you switch to affect ho w many credits will transfer to ward you new major. For information on switching majors, check with your academic advisor. You want to make sure that you're switch-ing for a good reason, that you have now selected a major that *is* a good fit for y ou, and that y ou understand ho w switching affects your current coursework and standings.

Now that y ou kno w some of the r eal tr uth about picking a major , let's look at some of the r esources you can use to help y ou decide on your major.

How to Decide

When considering what major to pursue, consider these guidelines:

1. **Look at your interests.** What do y ou like to do? What ar e your hobbies? How do you like to spend your time? What extracurricu-lar activities do or did y ou participate in? What have you enjoyed most? What hav e been y our fav orite subjects in school? What recurring skills have played a role in your success? When you fanta-size about your ideal career, what is that job like?

2. **Consider your abilities.** Think about y our natural talents. What do others say y ou ar e good at? Consider ho w your abilities align with y our inter ests. I f y ou hav e gr eat talent in an ar ea but z ero interest, choosing a major based on y our abilities isn 't going to make you happy. Likewise, if you have great interest in a topic, but zero abilities, your choice of a major may limit you.

3. **Reflect on your values.** What do y ou v alue? F inancial success? Spirituality? H elping others? E ntertaining others? I f y our car eer and study choices ar e in conflict with y our v alues, y ou will hav e problems. O n the other hand, if y ou choose a major (and then a

career) that are in alignment with what you value, you will improve your chances for happiness.

4. **Think about what it takes to make it in this major and whether you have what it takes.** Do you have the skills? motivation? ability? D oes the major r equire an adv anced degr ee? internships? Think not only about the academic challenges, but also about the financial costs and requirements.

5. **Look at the career opportunities in this field.** This topic is covered in detail Chapter 6, and Chapter 7 also provides some detailed case studies about people who hav e effectively used their E nglish degrees to pursue r ewarding car eers. You may also want to check out the r esearch section of y our librar y for publications, such as the *Occupational Outlook Handbook.* This r esource explains the requirements, salaries, and typical tasks of a number of jobs.   You can also find links to this r esource online at the B ureau of Labor Statistics (www.bls.gov).

6. **Honestly assess your reasons for choosing a major.** If you choose a major because it 's a good way to meet girls, bad idea. I   f y ou choose a major simply because y ou've heard it's "easy," that's also not a good r eason. If you choose a major because y ou think it has great money potential—wrong answer! If you choose to become an English major because y our dad was an E nglish major, ar e y ou choosing based on y our preference or y our dad's? If you are pressured by your family or peers, you'll likely end up unhappy. If you choose a major because a job market is currently hot, that's another wrong reason. What is the right reason(s) then? It's simple: Choose your major based on your interests and abilities.

Steven R othberg, pr esident of the M   inneapolis-based Web site CollegeRecruiter.com (www .collegerecruiter.com), r ecommends that students not focus on compensation or employment rates when picking a major. Instead, he says, "I f students focus on what they 're good at, what they like to do, and what's important to them, there's an excellent chance that they will end up in a job upon graduation that will make them happy."

RESOURCES

Although you don't want to allow someone else to make your decisions for y ou, y ou do hav e sev eral r esources to narr ow or confirm y our choice. These additional resources include:

♦ Talking to school counselors (at your high school and at prospective colleges).

♦ Using I nternet r esources such as inter est and personality testing (covered in Appendix A).

♦ Checking your potential college for resources. Some colleges provide aptitude testing to help y ou decide on a major . I ndiana University/Purdue University Indianapolis (IUPUI), for example, publishes a booklet called *Step Ahead to Your Future: a guide to choosing majors & careers* (IUPUI, U niversity College A dvising Center and Car eer Center). This step-by-step guide asks y ou to focus on y ourself and indicate ar eas of inter est. F rom this self-assessment, you can determine y our interest themes, skill pr eferences, and personality type. Armed with this information, y   ou can then target specific majors (and car   eers) that match y   our assessment, and you can explore and determine a realistic picture of the car eers and majors y ou have targeted as ar eas of inter est. You can ask for guides like this at your campus career center.

♦ Taking adv antage of the wor   kshops and online information offered by some schools.

♦ Trying the online personality or character testing some schools offer to provide guidance on choosing a major.

♦ Taking adv antage of internships or v   olunteer oppor tunities in your field.

♦ Talking to people who currently work in your field of interest.

♦ If you are already in college, taking classes in the potential major. Although you don't want to spend too many cr edit hours exploring majors, you can choose a few classes. You can also ask to sit in on classes (rather than formally enr oll). As another option, y ou can review the syllabus and course materials for a class and talk to professors who teach a class you're interested in.

A Closer Look at an English Major

Now that you know generally how to evaluate your choice of a major, let's take a closer look at what y ou can expect fr om this major . The following sections answer a host of questions, including the follo wing: What type person is generally suited for this major?   What ar e the requirements for this major?   What courses will y ou be taking?   What skills will you develop? What are the benefits of this major?   What are the challenges?

A QUICK SURVEY: IS ENGLISH RIGHT FOR YOU?

A few simple questions help y ou determine whether E nglish is a good major for you:

- ◆ Do you enjoy reading a wide variety of texts (not just one genr e, like mysteries or poetry, but a variety)?

- ◆ Do you like thinking, analyzing, and talking about what y ou've read?

- ◆ Do you enjoy expressing yourself in writing?

- ◆ Do you like arguing effectively to prove a point?

If you answer yes to these questions, your personality is probably suited for an E nglish major. If you answ ered no, y ou may want to consider other options or think about your motivation for choosing English as a major.

WHAT ARE THE REQUIREMENTS?

In the past, an E nglish major meant the study of the masterpieces of British and American literature. That definition doesn't suit today's college courses and English programs; now an English major encompasses a much br oader spectr um of topics and courses. A t the cor e, most English departments emphasize the following:

◆ Analyzing literature, a pr ocess that r equires critical thinking and logic

◆ Exploring your creativity and imagination

◆ Understanding differ ent cultur es and civilizations fr om v arious time periods and places

While the pr eceding skills ar e emphasiz ed, what course work y ou take—that is, the specific r equirements to graduate with a degr ee in English—will vary depending on your college and also the specific con-centration or specialty you pursue (see the upcoming section "Should I Specialize?"). F or example, literatur e-based studies usually focus on classical authors and time periods. Rhetorical studies, on the other hand, concentrate on communication skills in a v ariety of professional fields. Let 's consider the course work for a literatur e-based E nglish major first, and then look at some areas of specialization.

LITERATURE-BASED STUDIES

The most common type of English major is based on literature course-work and usually encompasses several time periods (such as Victorian), places (such as Great Britain), writers (such as Shakespeare), and genres (such as poetr y). You usually hav e a lot of choices in what classes y ou take. For example, you might expect to take the follo wing classes for a literature-based English degree:

◆ **Two courses in writing or composition and, quite possibly, one course in grammar:** You may, depending on the college and on y our writing skills, test into an adv anced writing or honors class (and possibly get cr edit for any writing classes that y ou test out of).

◆ **An introductory course in studying literature and another focused on rhetorical analysis:** The first course teaches y ou the basics of ho w to r ead a literatur e text critically as w ell as ho w to interpret and find meaning, wher eas the rhetorical analysis class focuses on the same skills, but considers nonfiction texts.

◆ **Several courses in American literature:** You may be required to take one overview or survey course as well as a choice of courses based on a variety of time periods (pre–Revolutionary War 1830 to 1941, 1941 to pr esent, for example), authors (H awthorne, Frost, H emingway), schools, mo vements (N aturalism or Transcendentalism), or genres (poetry, drama, and so on).

◆ **Several courses in British literature:** Like American literatur e, you may take a survey course as well as other courses based on time periods (the M iddle Ages, R omanticism), authors (S hakespeare, Chaucer), or genre.

◆ **One or more advanced writing courses:** Expect to take at least one other writing course. Examples include business communication, fr eelance writing for magazines, cr eative writing (fiction, nonfiction, poetr y, scr eenwriting, playwriting), writing for children or young adults, report and proposal writing, writing for the Web, and technical communications.

◆ **One or more courses in women's or multicultural literature:** Plan to take at least one course that focuses on women writers or writers from another culture. For example, you may take a survey course of women's literature, African American literatur e, Jewish literature, Irish literature, or Latino literature.

◆ **Several elective English courses:** In addition to taking classes that fall under certain categories, you'll also be able to select other English courses. I n addition to American, B ritish, and multicultural literature, y ou may be able to take courses in world literature, literature in translation (South Asian literature, the works of Dante, the no vels of D ostoyevsky), or courses on a par ticular genre (drama, folklore, the eighteenth century novel, and so on).

In addition to this course work, y ou'll also need to complete other specified courses. For example, most colleges require you to take related history courses (for example, mediev al history or the r enaissance), so that you can interpr et the literatur e you're r eading based on cultural and historical ev ents. You may also be r equired to take two or mor e courses in humanities and fine ar ts, as w ell as at least one y ear (often two) of a foreign language.

You'll also include courses for a minor or cer tification. (Chapter 3 covers selecting a minor or pursuing certification in more detail.) Finally, you may also have general degree requirements that include such areas as social sciences (anthr opology, sociology) and some basic math and science (but often not much, if any). F or exact r equirements, check with your particular school.

SHOULD I SPECIALIZE?

English majors at many universities may choose to concentrate in a particular area of specialization, such as literature (covered in the preceding section), creative writing, literary criticism, English language or linguistics, rhetorical studies, E nglish education, technical communication, and others. For example, some universities include film studies or children's literature as an ar ea of concentration within the E nglish department. In other schools, these depar tments may be their o wn distinct departments or areas.

If y ou kno w what y ou want to accomplish with y our E nglish degree, consider choosing one of these specialty ar eas. For example, if you want to be a writer, you may want to concentrate on creative writing. You'll take many of the same courses as a literatur e-based degree, but your coursework will also include several creative writing classes. If you want to focus on business communications or ar e planning to attend law school, consider focusing on rhetorical studies. I n this case, your classes will cover argumentative writing, history of rhetoric, visual rhetoric, as well as technical communication and editing classes. S ome colleges also offer a special technical communication concentration or degree that may or may not fall under the English department. For this type of specialty, plan to take classes similar to those offered for rhetorical studies.

As another option, you may plan to teach English. In this case, focus on E nglish education. F or example, P enn S tate U niversity allo ws for a secondary education option, thr ough which students obtain teaching

certification in communications and E   nglish. I f y ou pursue an
education-related English degree, in addition to taking basic literatur e
and writing classes, you'll be required to take advanced classes in linguistics; children's literature; and methods of teaching reading, writing, and
literature.

On top of these choices, many schools enable you to customize your
own concentration, selecting courses based on y our own unique interests and goals. Other schools permit students to work on an interdisci-
plinary major, combining English with another field.

As you can see, an E nglish major is not a one-siz e-fits-all approach.
You have plenty of opportunities to take classes that reflect your interests.

WHAT GENERAL SKILLS WILL I LEARN?

In addition to taking classes and learning specifically about English literature, criticism, and writing, this major also teaches and enhances
other life skills, which prepares you for a variety of jobs:

- ◆ Thinking critically

- ◆ Tapping into your creativity

- ◆ Expressing yourself in various types of writing

- ◆ Analyzing experiences from text or from life itself

- ◆ Appreciating the diversity of cultures as expressed through literature

- ◆ Questioning and exploring the human condition

WHAT CHALLENGES WILL I FACE?

One of the challenges for E nglish majors is r ealizing what E nglish is
and is not. Many students associate English with only one aspect of this
field—poetry or the classics, for example. But in reality there are a variety of options available, from nonfiction to Web pages, from film to the
history of language. And as an E nglish major, you need to appreciate a
variety of texts, not just one genre.

Another challenge is choosing a direction among the many different
paths. For example, an English major may pursue any number of types

of writing, including creative, nonfiction, business, technical, or medical writing, just to name a few.

Writing effectively may also be a challenge for some. English also doesn't have to equal writing, although that's clearly one of the skills you'll learn. You may also use your English major to communicate through the Web or in presentations or speeches. You can also use your English major to go onto a career in teaching or public relations.

Because English is not a career-specific major, when you graduate, you have to take the initiative to find a job you like. Contrast this to an accountant, for example, who studies solely to become an accountant and isn't left to ponder what type of job might suit that degree.

As an English major, you may not realize that you are qualified for lots of jobs, within and outside of the area of English—but you are! And the most successful English majors look at the opportunities early in their academic careers, and then make sure they attain the right skills and knowledge to succeed. That's the main purpose of this book: to make you aware of the various careers you can pursue with a degree in English.

The Job Outlook

In addition to thinking about classes, of course you want to know what jobs are and will be available for your major. The job possibilities are discussed in more detail in later chapters, but this section gives you a quick overview.

One of the most popular sources for job outlooks is the U.S. Department of Labor Bureau of Labor Statistics (www.bls.gov). Although this department doesn't have a category for "English majors," it does cover common careers, such as writers and editors. For these jobs, the U.S. Department of Labor Bureau of Labor Statistics lists these significant points:

- ◆ Employment in the communication sector is expected to increase by 16.9 percent by 2010. Through 2012, employment of writers and editors is expected to grow about as fast as the average for all occupations.

◆ Writers and editors held about 305,000 jobs in 2000. These jobs broke down into these categories: Writers and authors accounted for 126,000 jobs; editors held 122,000 jobs; and the r emaining 57,000 were technical writers.

◆ Nearly 25 per cent of the av ailable jobs for writers and editors were salaried positions with ne wspapers, magazines, and book publishers. M any—mostly technical writers—wor ked for computer software firms.

◆ Online publications and ser vices ar e exploding in number and complexity, making a demand for writers and editors, specifically those with Web expertise. Businesses and organizations ar e more commonly publishing ne wsletters and maintaining Web sites, adding jobs to create and maintain these publications.

◆ Because of the information explosion and rapid change in technical fields, expect many oppor tunities for technical writers, especially with expertise in law, medicine, economics, and technology. Today ther e's a gr eat need for writers to cr eate user's guides, instruction manuals, and training materials.

Many oppor tunities ar e available to y ou when y ou get a degr ee in English, whether y ou choose to go on to graduate school or immediately begin looking for a position after completing y   our four-y ear degree. This book pr ovides y ou with information on both of these options, as w ell as co vers how to choose a school (see Chapter 2) and get the most from your time at college (see Chapter 3).

Chapter 2

Choosing a College

In addition to thinking about what you want to study, you also need to think about *where* you will study; that is, what college will y ou attend? In making this decision, y ou consider factors r elated to y our personal situation, y our wants, and y our needs (for example, scholarship pr ograms, school location, school siz e, and so on). While you're evaluating each school overall, take a look at its E nglish department to ensure that it meets your needs.

This chapter focuses on the general considerations for choosing a college, as well as specific information to research when considering the English program. This chapter also co vers some tips on applying to a school.

Researching Colleges

Like selecting a major (see Chapter 1), y ou'll most likely get plenty of advice and feedback on choosing a college. You need to think about what college setting would be ideal for y ou, do y our r esearch, and weigh what you find with the advice y ou get from others. This section discusses some considerations when choosing a college.

HANDLING ADVICE

Everyone fr om y our par ents to y our gr eat-uncle J immy will offer an opinion about wher e y ou should attend school. P erhaps one of y our parents wants you to go to his alma mater. Your mother may want you to choose a school close to home, whereas you may want to venture to a place you've never been. Or, conversely, a parent may encourage you to attend a school a little farther from home if he or she thinks you need to expand your experiences. In addition to your family, your friends may also have an impact on your decision.

If you're in your junior or senior year of high school, "Where are you going to college?" is likely the main topic of conversation among your friends. Your friends may voice their opinions on your choices and may even influence that decision; you may decide to go to the same school as a friend, a group of friends, or a boyfriend or girlfriend.

You have a lot of factors to consider, but remember that everyone is different. The school that's best for you isn't necessarily the best school for your best friend. You both are likely seeking a unique experience; therefore, it's up to you to determine what factors are important in your ideal school, and then see how closely the schools you've identified match.

Your high school advisor may also have some suggestions for you, based on your academic performance and interests. He or she may suggest a few good schools to consider. Because your high school advisor knows what classes you have taken and how well you have done, he or she is a good source of advice. You can discuss your goals for college and see what schools your advisor recommends.

If you're a returning student, you won't be worried about where your high school friends are going! And you won't have as much pressure from peers and family. You'll likely choose a local college, one offering classes that are convenient to your schedule. See the "Returning to School" section for more advice on this situation.

REVIEWING COLLEGE BROCHURES AND INFORMATION

Some time in your junior year, you'll likely start to get letters and brochures from a number of colleges. The mailings will increase as your senior year starts. In addition to those unsolicited college packets, write and request information from the colleges that interest you most.

(Usually, you can visit the school 's Web site and r equest a packet of information.) You can also find information at the college 's Web site; use this information when you want to delve deeper into your information search.

For all the br ochures you r eceive (solicited and unsolicited), take time to look them o ver, so that y ou get a good idea of ho w a school markets itself. The materials each college includes helps y ou see what's important to that school.   What do they pr omote? G raduation rate? Student activities? Athletics? You get an o verall sense of the school and its priorities from its promotional materials.

Read thr ough each br ochure and highlight items of inter est. F or example, if y ou plan to par ticipate in a sor ority or fraternity, does this school offer them? D oes the college offer intramural athletic teams or community theater, if those interest you? Are recreational opportunities available in the town or surrounding area? Is the level of academic rigor appropriate for y ou? Look for other facts or figur es that stand out to you, depending on your areas of interest.

One key consideration is looking at the quality and oppor tunities in English. The college y ou ultimately choose should hav e an E nglish program that meets all y our academic and car eer goals. S ee the "Looking into the E nglish Program" section, later in this chapter , for more information.

Your goal as y ou review this material is to narr ow your list to a fe w schools. Then, if at all possible, visit these colleges—reading about and seeing a school are completely different experiences. By visiting a campus, you see the types of students who attend, wher e they live, what the classrooms are like, and so on. While there, try to talk to enr olled students and see whether they can r ecommend the univ ersity. You may ask the admissions office to giv e you some referral names (current students or r ecent graduates) to call and talk about their experiences at that school.

MAKING YOUR DREAM LIST

Coming up with schools y ou might attend is easy; as y ou see, just ask anyone and y ou'll get an opinion. Although y ou shouldn't make y our decision based on what someone else says, using the advice to come up with your initial list of possible colleges is fine.   You want to consider and explore a lot of possibilities befor e narrowing your choice to one. It's much better to, say, look into a school and decide it's located too far away, costs too much money, or has a reputation for too much partying on your own than have a parent insist this same point.

So make a list of all the colleges y ou're considering attending. Then gather the information about them to learn mor e about each college and its programs.

Start with an overview of all the colleges and think about where you ideally would like to go. Consider all colleges, even those that may turn out to be a terrible fit for you, so that you consider the range of colleges that are available. If you're interested in attending Harvard, consider it. Later, when y ou calculate the tuition, consider ho w far it is fr om your home, and take into account the high academic standar ds, y ou may realize that Harvard isn't really at all the best place for you.

Think about making a grid of the schools y ou are considering and include the criteria that ar e most impor tant to y ou. For example, y ou can include the tuition, miles from home, school reputation, likelihood of y our getting accepted, scholarship oppor tunities, and pr ograms of study. You can then complete each of these sections to see ho w each school stacks up against the others.

MAKING THE FINAL DECISION

When making a final decision, the following key questions or issues can help determine your choice:

- ◆ **What do your parents think?** For most students, parents pay for part or all of the college tuition, so although you shouldn't feel as if you have to go to the one and only school they select, consider their suggestions and reservations about colleges you're considering.

- ◆ **How much does the college cost?** When figuring the cost per year, don't forget to include tuition, books, housing, food, and travel to and from home. Out-of-state schools cost more than in-state schools; private schools are usually more expensive than public schools.

◆ **What financial opportunities does the school provide?** Are you eligible for any scholarships (academic, athletic, alumni, local)? A good Web site for checking into scholarship opportunities is www.fastweb.monster.com. Also, are you eligible for financial aid? What about student loan programs? Your high school advisor can provide information about financial aid; you can also get information about different aid packages from the schools you are considering.

◆ **How many students attend the school?** Of that number, how many live on campus? You may decide you want a smaller, more close-knit college, or you may want the experience of a large, major university.

◆ **How many students graduate? How many go on to graduate school?** The numbers not only give you a sense of the size of the school, but also an idea of the success of those students. A good school should be able to tell you what its graduates are currently doing—that is, it takes an active interest in their lives, instead of just graduating them and sending them out the door.

◆ **How far away from home is the school?** Depending on your personality, you may be very independent and have no problems going to school across the country. But if you're likely to want to visit home and your high school friends several times a year, take the distance into consideration. Is it an easy drive? Or will coming home require flying or taking a train?

◆ **What is the reputation of the school?** Is it accredited? You may ask your academic advisor about additional information. Consider also reviewing the college Web site, as well as recent articles in the paper about the school. (Use a search tool such as Google to search for stories in the news.) You can also find guides updated each year, such as *Princeton's Guide to Colleges* or *U.S. News & World Report America's Best Colleges;* these provide an overview of schools. (These guides often include other factors, such as ho w the school ranks accor ding to cer tain criteria or whether the school is known as a party school).

You'll find several publications that rank schools, citing those that are best. Although these can be a good r esource for ev aluating a school and its r eputation, keep in mind that these publications tend to focus on I vy League and other large, pr estigious schools. Just because a school isn't listed (or isn't ranked high on these lists) doesn't mean it's not a good school. Look at any rankings with some skepticism.

◆ **Do students and graduates recommend it?** Consider talking to current students, r ecent graduates, and alumni to get their ideas about the school. What did they like? What did they str uggle with? Are they friendly when they talk to you? Are they interested in having y ou attend that school? I f you don't talk with students on a visit or are unable to visit, ask the admissions office for refer-rals of current students or recent graduates. These people can give you the best sense of what the school is like fr om a student 's perspective.

Looking into the English Program

Identifying schools y ou may want to attend and determining the gen-eral characteristics are just par t of selecting a college. You also need to make sur e the school has a quality E nglish program. You can use the following questions and suggestions to help ev aluate the E nglish department and its program:

◆ **Does the department have a program that matches what you want to do?** For example, if you want to do creative writing, does the depar tment offer sev eral sections of cr eative writing classes? Does it have a special major within English for creative writing so that y ou can specializ e? The bottom line is this: M ake sur e the English department has a program that suits your specific interests.

English department offerings can vary, from a traditional focus on the classics and cer tain authors or time periods to something more innovative. For example, at some schools, you may be able to specialize your major, focusing on nonfiction writing, creative writing, film studies, or other types of English-related studies.

Keep in mind that if you aren't sure what path you want to choose, you want to choose a school that offers a variety of choices. Some schools, especially smaller schools, may focus on a few narrow or very broad areas of study.

◆ **What is the pedigree of the faculty?** Do faculty members have terminal degrees (that is, have they finished their doctorates or master of fine arts degrees)? Has the faculty won any teaching awards? Is the faculty still active in publishing and research? On one hand, you may want the opportunity to explore publishing and research with a professor. On the other hand, you don't want a professor who is so wrapped up in his or her own publishing career that he (or she) isn't an effective teacher or is unavailable. You can get information about professors from the college Web site. Or ask at your interview or school visit.

◆ **Who teaches the classes?** If the faculty is busy with research and publishing, you may have adjunct faculty or graduate students doing the bulk of teaching. This isn't necessarily a bad thing; often, the adjunct faculty are very good and have real-world experience. But if you select a college because you want to study with a particular professor, make sure that professor personally teaches the classes. Also, look for diversity in the instructors so that you get a variety of perspectives and experiences when pursuing your English degree. To find this information, check current course schedules (usually available online) to see who is listed for the classes you are considering. You can also see how many classes a certain professor teaches by scanning through the listings, looking for his or her name.

◆ **What classes are actually offered?** Look at the course catalog *and* the course schedule (both are usually available online). Some courses may be listed in catalog, but may not be offered very frequently. If you're interested in a particular class or set of classes, be sure that they are offered regularly.

◆ **What is the student to faculty ratio?** Will you be able to get individual attention and advice? This consideration is especially important when you need help landing an internship or shado wing a professional in the field, or if y ou're seeking a mentor (all topics covered in Chapter 3). O ne good test is whether y ou can make contact with someone in the English department (versus meeting with someone in the admissions office) when you are applying to or evaluating the school. I f a faculty member isn't available for a 15-minute meeting with y ou as y ou're shopping for a college, chances ar e that pr ofessors won't be r egularly av ailable to y ou when you're a student there.

◆ **What activities, organizations, and clubs does the English department or school support?** At the school's Web site, check out the page for the E nglish depar tment and get a sense of the opportunities available. For example, if you are interested in film studies, does the school hav e a film club? I f you are interested in creative writing, does the school have a literary magazine?

◆ **What type of college and career advising is available and who does the advising?** Professors in the English department? College or career advisors? Does the school hire professional advisors? Use peer advisors? A combination? What background do these counselors have? You want someone who has experience working in that field, which is usually going to be a faculty member . Professional advisors also pr ovide helpful information, especially r egarding which classes y ou need in or der to graduate. S tudents or peer advisors may provide a student perspective of the major, which is worthwhile when thinking about y our major or dealing with problems that occur with your major. You want someone who has experience working in that field. That may be the faculty, outside consultants, or ev en pr ofessional advisors. O ther types of counselors can also provide helpful information: Students or peer advisors, for example, may pr ovide a student 's perspectiv e of the major, which is wor thwhile when thinking about y our major or dealing with problems that occur with y our major. Look for this information on the depar tment's Web site. I f it's not av ailable there, ask during your campus visit.

- **What are classes like?** Visit some English classes, if possible. How active are the students? How effective is the professor? Would you be challenged by this class? Would you want to take this class? I f you sit in on two classes and find both to be boring or disorganized, you may want to consider another college and/or major.

- **Does the English department have a course that will help you determine what you can do with degree in English?** This type of course is becoming mor e popular because it not only sho ws students what is possible with a degr ee in E nglish, but also lets them know what skills and experiences they need to get *during* college in order to get that job after graduation.

- **Does the department track where their alumni are employed or where they have gone to graduate school?** A department that is committed to the success of its students often follows up to see how well they ar e doing in the r eal world—versus patting them on the back and letting them go after graduation.

Where can y ou find this information? B y reading through depart ment publications. You can also find information on the college Web site, b y talking with those in the E nglish depar tment, b y talking to other students, and by talking to faculty.

Applying to College

After y ou narr ow y our list of colleges, y ou make y our applications. Schools v ary, but most r equire scor es fr om a college entrance exam (either the SAT or the ACT, depending on the school), a college application, and y our transcripts fr om high school. O n the application, you'll most likely be asked to list y our high school activities. E ven if years have passed since you were in high school (and, if so, the follo wing section is just for y ou), think har d about y our inv olvement in school, athletics, work, and hobbies and be sure to include all of them. However, just because you weren't class president or the quarterback on the football team doesn 't mean y ou don 't hav e applicable skills and experiences that y ou can use to illustrate y our qualities. P erhaps y ou worked par t-time thr oughout high school. I   f so, what w   ere y our responsibilities? Look for skills y ou used on the job that apply to the rigor of English classes you'll take in college. Also include any v olunteer work or service hours you completed.

You'll also have to write a letter or essay, perhaps answering a specific question. S pend considerable time on this element. O   rganize y our thoughts, make clear points, edit and proofread for mistakes, and ask a teacher to giv e you feedback on it. Think of this as one of y our most important graded writing assignments! As a futur e English major, you have to submit a stellar admissions essay.

You may also attend an admittance inter view or have to meet other requirements to apply. In an interview, you may be asked why you want to attend that school, what extracurricular activities y   ou have participated in, whether you worked during school, and what major or career you plan to pursue. The interview is also a good opportunity for you to ask questions. F or example, y ou can ask about the E   nglish pr ogram, making sure it meets your career goals. You can also ask about guidance counseling, the size of the school, peer mentors, or any other questions you may have.

Many schools allow you to apply online (and to track y our application online). Check with your high school guidance counselor for help with application questions. I f your counselor can't help, check the college's Web site, which may include a list of fr equently asked questions about applications. And if y   ou're still stumped, call the admissions office directly. You want to make sure your application isn't overlooked or dismissed because y   ou forgot or incorr ectly filled out a r   equired element.

According to *U.S. News & World Report,* colleges emphasize, in order, these factors when deciding on admission:

- ◆ Grades in college prep courses

- ◆ Standardized admission tests

- ◆ Grades in all courses

- ◆ Class rank

- ◆ Essay or writing sample

- Teacher recommendation
- Counselor recommendation
- Interview
- Work/extracurricular activities
- Student's demonstrated interest in school

Special College Situations

If y ou're r eturning to college or transferring fr   om another college, review the advice in this section to help with your particular situation.

RETURNING TO COLLEGE

If you're returning to college fr om work or fr om raising a family , you need to go thr ough the same pr ocess of deciding which criteria define an ideal college for y ou, researching colleges, looking into the E nglish department, and applying for college. Your choices may be mor e lim-ited because of family , wor k, location, or financial concerns, but y ou still want to choose the best school for you.

Depending on your situation, you may have different needs or stress different aspects of the college envir onment. For example, if y ou have young childr en, y ou may want to see whether the school offers day-care facilities for par ents. I f you're wor king and going to school, look for a school that has flexible class scheduling, such as night courses. Some schools offer these classes off-campus at convenient sites, such as high schools or shopping malls. You may also look into online schools, but be sure they are accredited. (Every Web site should explicitly state whether a school is accredited. If you aren't sure, ask.) You may want a school with a div erse student body (perhaps with older or r   eturning students rather than just the typical students aged 18 to 22 years old).

If you're returning to college and hav e taken college courses in the past, check with the admissions office at each school you're considering to see whether the cr edits can still be applied to ward y our degree. At many schools, credits expire after a certain number of years.

TRANSFERRING TO A NEW COLLEGE

If y ou ar e considering transferring to a ne w school, go thr ough the same process of identifying and selecting a new college. Because you've already been to college, think about what worked and what didn't work about your last college experience. Why are you transferring? What are you seeking in your new school?

As for the classes y ou have already taken, check with admissions to see whether the credits will transfer. This may take some haggling. F or example, you may have to show how two classes (one from each school) are essentially the same, although they have different names. Try to find an ally on your new campus who can help steer you through the transfer pr ocess, perhaps an admissions office, an advisor , or an E nglish department faculty member.

Making the Most of Your Time at College

Your time at college will go b y quickly, and if y ou think that studying the material and making decent grades is enough to land you a gr eat job, you want to r ethink your appr oach. Employers don't really care whether you can recite a timeline of Russian novels and their authors (unless y ou're going to be hir ed as a R ussian literatur e professor); they car e about what y ou've experienced, perhaps writing a senior thesis sho wing y our effectiv e writing style, perhaps doing research, perhaps being a mentor to incoming students. What you get involved in and what y ou do with y our time are just as impor tant—if not more so—than the content you learn in the classes you take.

That's not to say that y ou shouldn't study or learn the material in your classes; what it does say is that if y ou want to graduate and get a job or go on to graduate school, you have to start making plans during your entire college career, not just that last year or semester. This chapter focuses on the many ways that as an E nglish major y ou can maximize y our college experience so that y ou can find success when y ou finish your degree. (Chapters 4 and 5 cover where to find and continue that success, whether in graduate school or the working world.)

This chapter focuses on getting the most fr om your classes, exploring car eer possibilities early in y our college experience, and taking advantage of real-world opportunities such as internships and job shadowing. (For more about networking after college, see Chapter 5.)

Planning Your Classes

Most employers and graduate programs aren't interested in the content you know. They want to know what skills you have acquired; in particular, what social skills. Can y ou work with a team? get along with a diverse group of people? take the initiative? be persistent? (This follows the same list of characteristics that most employers seek; this list is covered in Chapter 5.)

The most important goal is to have some understanding of what job you want to do. Your major coursework will be determined by the path you select, but you can then add to this kno wledge by a careful choice of a minor and electiv es. For example, if y ou want to use y our English degree to get a job in adv ertising, you might wor k toward a minor in advertising or take courses in mar keting research and analysis. I f you want to use your English degree to work in advertising, you may want to take marketing and advertising courses.

If you aren't sure what skills a particular path requires, look into it in more depth. (Chapters 5 and 6 intr oduce some common and not-so-common paths pursued b y English majors; Chapter 7 shar es real-life stories of sev eral English majors.) You can also ask y our college car eer department or depar tment advisor for advice. I f they kno w what y ou are interested in, these pr ofessionals can guide y ou toward classes that fit that interest and build particular skills. Faculty members are another great resource for making r ecommendations on minors or other electives to take as part of your complete degree.

DOUBLE MAJOR?

Should you get a double major? Only if you think it's critical to succeed in the particular field you are interested in. For example, if you want to teach English as a second language, y ou'd position y ourself well upon graduation by pursuing an additional major in a language (Spanish, for example). A foreign language degree is also useful in international business or government.

If you don't pursue a double major, carefully select your minor. Your minor is an extra set of kno wledge (thr ough an extra set of r equired classes) that is concentrated in one area and enables you to gain skills in a relevant area. For example, if you want to pursue a writing career, you may decide to minor in journalism to gain more writing experience.

Science and technology ar e also good candidates for double majors or minors. I n fact, combining science and E nglish pr ovides many opportunities and even scholarships. You may use this combination to pursue a car eer in medical writing, a specializ ed field that r equires a good understanding of science.

Likewise, a technology backgr ound may open doors for a technical writing car eer. I t's not necessarily kno wing a par ticular pr ogram, but being able to cr eate intelligent text (documents and Web pages, for example) with modern technology that is impor tant. If you have cr eativity and critical thinking skills but lack technical skills, you may lose out to someone who does have those skills.

You may also determine whether y our college offers cer tificates in different subjects (for example, editing, journalism, or technical writing). These cer tificates are awarded b y outside organizations based on required course work and some outside ev aluation or assessment (a portfolio of y our writing, for example). G etting a cer tificate usually requires more credit hours than a minor, but it provides an outside recommendation based on y our o wn wor k, which may be appealing to employers.

The bottom line is that y ou won't find a magical combination of classes/majors/minors for English majors. There's just the combination that's right for you and what you want to pursue.

WRITING A SENIOR THESIS

Your pr ogram may r equire y ou to write a senior thesis. This r equirement v aries fr om pr ogram to pr ogram and fr om school to school. Know the exact requirements of your major from the very beginning so that something big—like a senior thesis—doesn 't sneak up and take you by surprise!

A senior thesis is especially important if you plan to pursue graduate school, because it's an independent experience that shows good research and writing skills.

Some ways to use y our senior thesis to help pr epare for y our future in English include writing y our thesis on y our career field or writing a thesis that involves research or synthesis on a key issue r elated to your career of interest. For example, suppose that you're interested in teaching abroad. What does it involve? Where are the challenges in this field right now? What are the job opportunities? What is the outlook? How is this field changing the way w e live? Answering these questions in a senior thesis not only creates an interesting paper but also lets you focus your school work on a useful topic—learning mor e about one of y our possible career interests.

In addition to your academic studies, look at the other opportunities to gain experience (and have fun and meet people) at your school.

Writing and Editing

If you plan to pursue a career as a writer, one of the most important ways you can build your résumé to is have some published work to your credit. You can look for opportunities to write and get your work published on campus or off. For example, your college most likely has a literary magazine. If you like creative writing, you may submit your work to this journal. I f you like nonfiction writing, y ou may find opportunities for publishing in your campus newspaper, Web site, or yearbook.

In addition to having y our writing published, if y ou want to be an editor, look for ways to get editing experience. S eek a staff position as an editor, writer, pr oofreader, lay out designer, Webmaster, or other position. All of these pr ovide you with r eal-world working experience as a writer or editor.

Your opportunities aren't limited to y our campus. You may publish articles in or edit a local chur   ch, club , or organization ne wsletter. Consider working for your daily hometown paper during the summer. You might also create and maintain a Web site for your church or club.

In all these instances, your goal is to have published work or relevant job skills to impress a potential employer or graduate school.

Joining Clubs and Organizations

Take advantage of the campus activities and organizations. Participating in activities and joining organizations help you meet others in the field (this is also called networking). You can also use campus activities as a chance to expand your experience, perhaps by participating in a club. These experiences also help you build skills useful for the job market. Even if they aren't related to English, these activities can be a bonus. If you're the events planner for your sorority and you want to work for a PR firm or in a nonprofit organization, for example, you can show how your event-planning skills are a perfect match for some requirements of those fields.

You may join a film club or a campus group such as Student Republicans or Young Democrats. You can also participate in student services, serving on the student government, for example. Your goal is to take a leadership role in some activity and use this to prove your initiative and drive.

Also, get involved in the English department's activities; these may include signing guest speakers, planning receptions and seminars, and working on committees. You may want to attend an academic conference that is held at your school or nearby.

Look into the English clubs or organizations on your campus and get involved. Specifically, check to see whether your school has a chapter of Sigma Tau Delta or any other English clubs. Sigma Tau Delta (see the Appendix) has activities to help students network with professors and professionals in the field. From these relationships, you may become involved in writing projects, complete an internship, shadow a job, and more. Those connections then become a good source of letters of recommendation for applying to graduate school or for applying to get a job. Also, you may submit papers for presentation at the annual convention or for publication in Sigma Tau Delta's journal, the *Rectangle.* You can visit the society's Web site at www.english.org for information about chapters and membership.

As another possibility for gaining experience, your English department may have part-time employment opportunities. Another idea is to check with the career center for job or volunteer opportunities; you may want to be a mentor to new students, for example. Or you may work for the college Web site, answering e-mail questions or creating articles for the site.

As you can see, clubs and campus activities offer some great ways to get involved. When you apply to graduate school or for a job, you can use these experiences to sho w off the skills, characteristics, or kno wl-edge you gained from these experiences.

Internships, Volunteering, and Part-Time Work

In addition to campus activities, look at mor e formal oppor tunities to explore differ ent car eers and gain experience.   These include intern-ships, volunteer work, and part-time work.

GETTING REAL-WORLD EXPERIENCE THROUGH AN INTERNSHIP

Internships are a key way to gain experience and information. Participating in an internship pr ovides you with r eal-world experience, making y ou more attractive to graduate schools or emplo yers. If you participate in an internship, you gain many benefits. F irst, the experience can help you fine-tune your career path. After participating in an internship, you may end up saying, "Yes, this is something I want to do!" On the other hand, the experience may end with your deciding, "I thought I wanted to be a journalist, but I don't like asking hard questions. This is not the career for me." It's much better to find out this information now rather than discover you're not suited for it after you graduate and pursue all the accreditation, advanced schooling, or job searching necessary to get you into a specific career.

In addition to enabling y ou to test-driv e a car eer, an internships gives you relevant job experience to include on y our résumé. You not only learn mor e about that par ticular field, y ou also gain a job r efer-ence. This leads to mor e benefits when you are seeking a job. If you par-ticipate in an internship, studies have shown you're more likely to find a job in that particular area, you're likely to receive more job offers after graduation, and you may r eceive a higher star ting salary when you do land a job . Try to par ticipate in at least one internship during y our undergraduate studies. To find out ho w, see the "F inding Internships, Volunteer, and Part-Time Opportunities" section.

DOING VOLUNTEER WORK AND WORKING

You may also consider doing v olunteer work. Like an internship , volunteer work gives you the chance to actually work in the field; this can
help you determine whether it's a field you want to pursue. Second, you
gain valuable experience. Third, you meet people who can add to your
network. Volunteering for any gr oup will add to y our résumé, but
the more specific to your chosen career path it is, and the more responsibilities you take on, the better . S ee the follo wing section for mor e
information.

You may also look for a part-time job that includes relevant skills. For
example, look for a job with the publication center for the university. You
might find a chance to work on university publications such as alumni
newsletters, Web sites, directories, marketing materials, and so on. Look
for part-time work positions within the English department as well.

FINDING INTERNSHIPS, VOLUNTEER, AND PART-TIME OPPORTUNITIES

You'll find ample oppor tunities for internships, v olunteer wor k, and
part-time work. The following gives you several resources to consider:

- ◆ Become a teaching assistance or take some r ole as a mentor for
  other students.   You can find these oppor   tunities as both an
  undergraduate and graduate student. F or example, y ou may volunteer at your campus writing center to help other students with
  their writing skills.

- ◆ Ask to assist a pr   ofessor in his or her r   esearch, writing, or
  other projects, either as an intern, v olunteer, or par t-time (paid)
  assistant.

- ◆ Check with y our career center, which will usually hav e information about internships and par   t-time wor k. I n addition to the
  department, look at the school level. For example, you may check
  into the school of liberal arts (usually the encompassing school for
  English) for internship or work opportunities.

◆ Use your library and find one of the many guides to internships, including *The Internship Bible, Best 110 Internships* and *Peterson's Internship Guide,* which list internships by field and include general information, benefits, and contact information.

◆ Visit Web sites to check for internships, volunteer opportunities, or summer/part-time work. You may look by area, organization, or career. For example, if you're interested in using your English degree in connection with politics (as a lobb yist, for example), you may want to find an internship in   Washington, D.C. Try these sites: www.dcinternship.org, www.twc.org, and www.washingtoninternship.com. If you want to use y our English major to work with y outh dev elopment agencies, visit the N   ational Assembly, which provides a directory of internships in these agencies (www.nassembly.org).

◆ If y ou're inter ested in wor king for a par ticular company, check with that company . M any company Web sites list internships. You can also call the human r esources depar tment to ask about opportunities.

◆ If you're interested in a job in publishing, check out the job postings at M edia B istro (www.mediabistro.com), which lists many paid and unpaid internships in N ew York City and ar ound the country. You hav e to r egister y our name and passwor d for this site, but you don't have to pay and can opt out of getting e-mail from them.

◆ Check with the car eer center or alumni association at y our college. Many alumni, typically an underused resource, volunteer to be mentors, to pr ovide shadowing oppor tunities, or to schedule information interviews about their career. In addition to mentoring and information, they may also be able to help y ou find an internship or part-time job.

◆ Check out not-for-profit organizations. These organizations often use interns as temporar y staffing. To find not-for-pr ofits, check out online r esources, look in the Yellow P ages, and check with your local chamber of commer ce to see whether they hav e any internship or v olunteer oppor tunities. You might, for example, work on a mar keting campaign for a not-for-pr ofit, cr eating brochures or letters to solicit help.

Networking While in School

When you're in college, begin to explor e your various car eer paths of interest. You can learn more about a career by getting information from your career center, but often the best place for information is from people who actually per form that type of job . You can take adv antage of resources at the car eer center and y our school to star t networking while you're still in school. Doing so provides you with the opportunity to learn mor e about differ ent car eers as w ell as to make impor tant connections.

FINDING PEOPLE IN YOUR FIELD

You have several sources available for finding people who work in your field of interest and who can help you learn more about finding a career with an English degree. First, start at your school's career center, which should have access to employers and alumni, as well as to students who have recently participated in an internship or have recently found work. You can identify jobs of inter est (if y ou already have some idea of the career you want to pursue) and see whether the career center can find a match. Or you can ask the career center to put you in touch with people who graduated with an English degree and are now working.

Alumni, for example, are a great source for information. You share a connection with these people: y our school! They are likely to want to help you. You can ask them for information about car eers of inter est. Or ask y our school for a list of alumni with E nglish degr ees and see what jobs they curr ently hold. R utgers, for example, lists r ecent grad-uates in E nglish as w ell as their job titles on its   Web site (www . rutgers.edu).

Other sour ces include pr ofessors, y our par ents, friends of par ents, and parents of friends. All these people ar e sources of networking con-nections. From these sources, you might be able to shadow a job, set up an information interview, and even find a mentor.

JOB SHADOWING

One way to investigate a career to see whether you like it and to make valuable connections is to job shado w. Your school may hav e some organized job shado wing pr ograms. F or example, jobshado wing is common in medical and dental school. Check with y our career center to see whether it has a list of practicing pr ofessionals who are available for shadowing. If your career center doesn't have a job shadowing program or list, y ou may need to make the connections y ourself. I n this case, if you meet someone who has a career you think you might like to pursue, ask whether you can shadow him or her for a day (or a morning or afternoon). Most people are honored to help, and if they say no, you can try other people.

When shado wing, don 't inter fere with the person 's wor kday and schedule. R emain in the backgr ound, as an obser ver. You should, though, at some time get a chance to talk to that person about the job. (See the following section for more ideas about questions to ask.)

SCHEDULING INFORMATIONAL INTERVIEWS

When you make a connection with someone who has a job of inter est or who has put his or her E nglish degree to good use, be pr epared to ask that person questions, thr ough an informational inter view, to help you on your career path. You can also set up these informational interviews as a way to gather information (and make contacts) with those in the field.

Make sure, when you're talking about careers, that you're not asking the person for a job . Instead, focus on asking questions *about* the job. The following list gives you a good idea of the questions to ask:

◆ What are the promotions or paths from that field? How did you get your start? What did you do next? What went well in your career so far? What would you do differently if you could do it over?

◆ What do you like best about your job? What do you dislike?

◆ What ar e y our daily duties? wor k hours? What is a typical day like?

- What are people in this field like?

- What skills do you need to succeed in this career?

- What were the most positive career decisions you made?

- What were some of the challenges y ou faced and ho w did y ou overcome them?

- What books, journals, and Web sites are useful to prepare myself for a career in this field? What books, journals, and Web sites do you frequent?

- What other advice do y ou hav e for me to get star ted? What haven't I asked that I should hav e? Can you tell me someone else I might talk to?

After the interview, be sure to send a thank-you note, handwritten or typed (but not via e-mail, because this is too informal). Little courtesies like this go a long way in establishing a r elationship with the people that you meet in your career exploration.

FINDING A MENTOR

Through information interviews, by pursuing internships, and b y participating in activities, y ou may be lucky enough to hook up with a mentor. A mentor is someone, usually a professional already established in a par ticular field, who takes a special inter est in y ou and helps y ou make connections, arranges interviews and internships, gives you advice on what classes to take or wher e to go to graduate school, and after you've gotten to know each other, writes letters of recommendation.

Having a mentor can be like having a fair y godmother, so it's worth your effor t to seek a willing pr ofessional to help y ou. You can find a mentor by talking to faculty, working with your school's alumni office, or b y meeting someone while wor king an internship . (Keep in mind that many alumni hav e signed up to be mentors but ar e never called; this is an under used resource for finding a mentor .) Finally, you may simply identify someone after whom y ou want to model y our career and simply ask that person to be your mentor.

Chapter 4

Attending Graduate School in English

The decision about whether to attend graduate school depends on your aspirations. If you want to be teach English at the university level, for example, you must attend graduate school because a Ph.D. or MFA (master of fine ar ts) is required. On the other hand, if y ou want to work in advertising, you don't need an advanced degree.

This chapter looks at the oppor tunities graduate school offers, explains ho w to select a graduate school and pr ogram, and tells y ou how to apply for graduate school. F inally, this chapter discusses some specific r esources y ou can use to find additional information about these topics.

Master's Degrees Mean Money

According to the U.S. Census Bureau, if you have a master's degree, you can expect to earn, over your lifetime, an average of $400,000 more than someone with only a bachelor's degree. If you complete your doctorate, on average, you'll earn $1.3 million more (over your lifetime) than someone with only a bachelor's degree.

Planning for a Postgraduate Degree

If you plan to pursue graduate school, you need to do the following:

◆ Plan your coursework so that y ou take courses that will pr epare you for an advanced degree. See the "Selecting Your Undergraduate Coursework" section for more information.

◆ During y our junior y ear, star t r esearching graduate schools of interest.

◆ Take the GRE (G raduate Entrance Exam), both the general test and the E nglish literatur e specific subject exam. Check out the schedule for when and where this test is held as well as when you need to sign up. It's best to take this test in your junior year or by November or December of your senior year. Usually, you register two or three months before the test.

◆ Submit your application for graduate school.

You'll find more detailed information about each of these steps in this chapter.

Selecting Your Undergraduate Coursework

One of the criteria used to decide on your admission to graduate school is your coursework. For that r eason, it's important that y ou plan y our coursework *before* you apply to graduate school so that you have the best chance of getting into the school you want. Consider these suggestions:

◆ Take challenging course work. I f possible, take mor e than the required number of courses.

◆ If possible, do a research project or have some published examples of your work (see Chapter 3 for more information).

◆ If know what you want to specialize in, get a solid foundation in that area. For example, if y ou want to focus on B ritish literature, take as many classes (and related courses, such as British history) as you can.

◆ If you have a good idea of where you want to pursue your graduate degree, look up the requirements while you are still pursuing your undergraduate degree. Then plan your coursework so that it best illustrates how you have met the requirements of that school.

Selecting a School and Degree Program

If you're in college, you likely are already familiar with the steps on how to research a school. You follow the same basic procedure when looking into a graduate program that you followed when looking into your undergraduate school. Consider these strategies for finding information about the many available programs:

◆ Check out the school's Web site to see what the graduate program offers. Does it meet your needs? Does it have enough diversity or options? What if you change your focus? Is the program flexible?

◆ Look into the faculty at the college. Does the school include any key faculty? For example, if you are interested in a particular type of writing (nonfiction, creative, medical, for example), does the school have any experts in that field?

◆ Look at the activities of the faculty. What percentage of faculty are publishing? Are the programs you are interested in actively pursuing new information? You don't want to choose a program that is stagnant within that department.

◆ Ask your department head, a professor you admire at your college, any alumni, and all other networking connections for recommendations. For example, ask where your favorite professor pursued his graduate degree(s)? Ask what those schools were like.

◆ If possible, make a personal visit to the graduate schools that interest you. Also, talk to students in each school's graduate program.

- Look into mentoring and car eer advising r esources. Will y ou be able to find a mentor? internship? car eer advice? S ee what resources both the career center and the English department offer.

- Determine what activities and oppor tunities ar e av ailable for graduate students. D oes the campus hav e publishing oppor tunities, such as a creative magazine, newsletters, journals, newspaper, student Web site, or other publishing venues? What other graduate English activities are available?

- Visit sites dedicated to r eviewing or discussing graduate schools; for example, www.gradschool.com or www.graduateguide.com.

  www.gradschool.com includes links to graduate schools (mostly those with online graduate pr ograms). The GRE page contains links for test pr eparation sites (which charge fees). O n the other hand, G raduateguide.com enables y ou to sear ch for a school b y major or state. You can then review the list of schools and get information about each of the schools and its English graduate program.

- Make sur e y our graduate pr ogram and school ar e accr edited. (Graduateguide.com includes an ar ticle on the impor tance of accreditation as well as resources to find out whether your school is accredited.)

Getting in to Graduate School

Applying for graduate school is similar to applying for college, only the graduate school admittance committee is looking for an experienced, learned student. The stakes ar e higher, but the r equirements are very similar.

In par ticular, the gradate school will most likely r eview the following:

- **Your undergraduate grade point average (GPA) and your transcript:** The committee will look at what courses you took, whether you showed improvement over your school car eer, whether y our coursework has any gaps or holes, and whether y our coursework shows planning for your specific career.

◆ **Your scores on the GRE:** Generally, the GRE tests for general knowledge in math, logic, and language skills.   You'll especially want to concentrate on language skills, those that look for evidence of good v ocabulary and analysis of text.   You also take a component for your area of study. So for English, you'll take the English literature subject test, in addition to the general testing. This component tests y our kno wledge about E nglish subjects (authors, themes, classics, and so on) and pr ovides an oppor tunity for y ou to sho w off y our analysis skills when r eading and commenting on texts.

◆ **Your participation in other activities:** Were you involved in any clubs? Did you have any of your work published? Did you do any mentoring or volunteering? Did you participate in an internship?

◆ **Your statement or essay:** Usually, you express your thoughts on why you want to pursue this degr ee and also explain what skills you have. Make sure to look at all of y our experience and activities and cast them in a way that fits y our graduate school goals. For example, if y ou w ere the ev ents planner for y our fraternity, include this experience, even if it's not directly an "English" activity. (In this case, focus on the skills: planning large ev ents, advertising the event, maintaining a schedule, and so on.)

◆ **Letters of recommendation:** In Chapter 3, you're encouraged to network, volunteer, find a mentor , and/or get an internship . All of this work pays off when y ou can find r elevant people to write glowing letters of recommendation.

PREPARING FOR THE GRE

For this test, you can find a range of GRE test pr eparation, from expensive, intense study course to pr eparation books to sample examples. Although you may not need the intense study course, look into some preparation work so that you know what to expect. What types of questions does the test include? What topics are covered? Check out Wiley's extensive range of GRE test-pr eparation books at www.wiley.com. Also, look for books in your library, the career center at your school, and the bookstore. Also, check with your advisor; he or she may have resources for preparing for taking this exam.

GETTING LETTERS OF RECOMMENDATION

Your college work should help you network and meet others who can write effective letters of recommendation (see Chapter 3). These letters are most effective when you know what the graduate committee is looking for in such a letter.

You might ask someone on the faculty staff with experience in writing letters of recommendation for a generic copy of a recommendation letter or a list of skills that particular professor thinks are critical. You can then review the letter or list, pursuing these skills and building up evidence of these same skills. You can also use the letter or list to relate existing experiences, skills, and knowledge to these essential grad school qualities.

Also, when you ask someone to write a letter of recommendation, let him or her know what path you are pursuing and what you think are the important attributes to stress. Many people give the recommender a résumé. Finally, be sure to ask enough in advance to give the person time to compose the letter; three to four weeks is standard; less than that may be seen as impolite.

PAYING FOR GRADUATE SCHOOL

When you continue your schooling, you need to pay for your additional education. Even if your parents provided help with your undergraduate degree, they are more likely to expect you to pay for further studies.

You do have some avenues for pursuing financial help. First, apply for an assistantship. The role (and compensation) varies, and it's not great money, but it usually pays for your tuition and a small salary for food and housing. An assistantship might include teaching (or helping teach) certain introductory English courses, such as freshman composition. You may help the instructor grade papers, prepare for class, and so on. For other assistantships, you may do research. Check with the graduate department to apply for these opportunities.

You can find other financial resources in work study; private, federal, and state loans (when you enter graduate school, you become a "professional student" and the cap on loan amounts change); grants;

fellowships; tuition-remission programs; and merit-based aid awarded on academic accomplishment, talent, or pr omise. You can find these resources thr ough y our univ ersity as w ell as possible outside sour ces, such as the organizations listed in the Appendix.

Returning to School

You don't hav e to immediately go fr om undergraduate to graduate school. You may decide to pursue a career or a family, or you may need a break from school. You can then return to graduate school later, when you feel ready.

In this case, y ou'll follow the same steps as someone who's applying as an undergraduate: You'll submit your transcripts, take the GRE, get letters of recommendation, and submit an application.

As a returning student, consider these tips:

◆ **Renew any friendships or acquaintances you have from school.** You might visit or write to faculty sev eral months before your application is due. You basically ar e looking for candidates for your letters of recommendation.

◆ **Consider taking a few classes if you've been out of school for a while.** This will help p repare you for returning to school. I t may also refresh or r emind you of some of the basic information y ou need to know.

◆ **Decide how much help you need with the GRE.** It's usually best to take this while in college, when all the content y ou study is still fr esh in y our mind. I f y ou hav e been out of school for a while, y ou may need to pr epare mor e extensiv ely for the GRE with a study book or course.

◆ **When you write your essay or statement, account for your time away from school.** Even if you were staying at home with a young child or working at a dead-end job, look at the skills and accomplishments you gained from these experiences. Staying home with a young child may have taught you time management, for example. Try to present your experiences in a positive light that shows some connection or usefulness to the new path you are pursuing.

Pursuing Other Graduate Degrees

An advanced degree in English isn't the only path for English majors. It's not uncommon for potential law students, for example, to major in English. With its emphasis on critical thinking, pr oblem-solving, and persuasive argumentation in papers you write, English provides a solid preparation for law school. If you're interested in law school, you'll need to research the various law schools as well as prepare for that admittance test (the LSAT).

Another graduate degree that has become more popular is a master's in library science (MLS). Again, a major in English is good preparation for a car eer in managing or wor king in v arious types of libraries. Chapter 7 includes a case study of someone who took this path.   You can also find more information about pursuing this career by checking into library science programs at schools that are of interest to you.

Breaking into the Job Market with an English Degree

Times have changed; people no longer star t and end their car eers with one company, retiring after 25 or more years of service with that ubiquitous gold watch. In fact, the Bureau of Labor Statistics estimates that y ou'll hav e at least 9 differ ent jobs betw een college and retirement, but most r esearchers think this number is way too lo w! They estimate that you should plan on having 20 or more jobs. You can expect to not only switch jobs but also change career fields entirely over the course of y our wor king life. What else can y ou expect? E xpect to lose your job through no fault of your own. (Companies go out of business, merge, or do wnsize.) E xpect to make some mistakes in y our career. But that's jumping the gun. Let's take a step back and figure out how to get that job in the first place. This chapter shows you how.

Planning Ahead

To help y ou get a job after y ou graduate, follo w the suggestions in Chapter 3: participate in activities, get some of your writing published, work with a mentor , v olunteer, inv estigate car eers of inter est befor e your last semester in college or graduate school, and par ticipate in at least one internship . S tudents who follo w these guidelines ar e better prepared when applying for jobs.

If you do not take advantage of these opportunities, you won't be on the same lev el as those with actual experience. O ne thing to keep in mind, though, is that emplo yers and r ecruiters ar en't looking for job hires based on major. Instead, they are looking at skills and characteristics. According to the National Association of Colleges and Employers, the top 10 characteristics that emplo yers look for in pr ospective hires include (in order of importance):

1. Communication skills

2. Honesty/integrity

3. Teamwork skills

4. Interpersonal skills

5. Motivation/initiative

6. Strong work ethic

7. Analytical skills

8. Flexibility/adaptability

9. Computer skills (basic knowledge of common office applications)

10. Self-confidence

That means if y ou've made the most of y our college car eer, be sur e to stress these qualities in addition to your experiences, skills, and knowledge. If you didn't quite make the most of y our oppor tunities during college, still look for ways to illustrate the pr eceding qualities. F or example, perhaps you were a cheerleader. You can use this experience to show how you work well with a team as well as highlight your motivation skills. I f y ou w ere pr esident of y our fraternity, you can y our experiences as a communicator, leader, planner, and so on to show how that experience illustrated your mastery of these characteristics.

Preparing Your Résumé

You need a résumé when attending car eer fairs and applying for jobs. You can find entir e books on cr eating a winning résumé. This section summarizes some of the key points that are especially useful for finding jobs with an English major. Be sure to include the following character-istics in your résumé:

- ◆ Include all your pertinent contact information.

- ◆ Rather than list your career objective (the job you seek) at the top, begin with a list of y our key skills and experiences, which helps "sell" you. Highlight your key knowledge, experiences, and char-acteristics. Summarize why someone should hir e you. Succinctly include in a short list what you have to offer.

- ◆ Highlight any publishing, editing, or writing experiences, includ-ing internships, mentoring, v olunteer wor k, and so on. D on't just list the experience—for example, " Worked on y earbook, September 2005 to S eptember 2006." B ut go bey ond the specifics of the title and dates and explain what y ou did. S how what skills y ou learned or practiced fr om this experience: "Created layout designs. Edited and proofread text for accuracy."

- ◆ Be sure to "sell" all your activities, not just those related directly to English. Think of how you spent y our time and whether during your college car eer there's anything else wor th mentioning. F or example, perhaps during the summer, you worked as a temporary assistant, creating, editing, and pr oofing a variety of office docu-ments. O r perhaps y ou v olunteered for y our chur ch or some other organization ne wsletter. D on't just focus on the ob vious, but include anything even remotely relevant.

- ◆ Include any and all r elevant work experiences in addition to col-lege. Although some jobs may seem to hav e nothing to offer—such as selling ice cr eam at the mall—perhaps the fact that y ou started working at 15 to sav e money for college makes mention-ing that job worthwhile.

◆ When you relate your job tasks, r ecast them in business terms. Also, tie the job experience to that field specifically. For example, if you created a kiddie ne wsletter in y our job as summer camp counselor, include the ability to cr eate and publish appr opriate, informative types of communication. This information is useful if you're applying for a job in adv ertising or writing. Think about all of your experiences and make sure they highlight the key skills and abilities you mastered.

◆ Use the r esources at y our car eer center to pr epare y our résumé. The center is not only likely to hav e several books and examples in the librar y, but it also has car eer counselors who can critique and provide feedback on your résumé.

You may also consider having business car ds printed up with y our name and contact information. These ar e easy to pass out, especially when networking.

Finding a Job

When you've prepared your résumé and ar e ready to sear ch out a job , here's the hardest part: Where do you start looking?

When most people think of finding a job , they think of the traditional methods: classified ads, and mor e r ecently, the I nternet. B ut according to a recent article in *USA Weekend* about careers, "more than 85 percent of all jobs are in a hidden job market of unadvertised or created opportunities. That job market includes people hired from within the company and hir ed thr ough wor d of mouth (without adv ertising the position)."

This section discusses some traditional job-hunting strategies. After all, you don't want to ignore the paper entirely; even if the listings don't include a job of interest to you, you can see what types of jobs ar e being advertised. You can also take a look at the Internet, although you'll soon realize that the I nternet and its many job posting sites ar e not the perfect solution. Finally, this section looks at some other, more promising, ways to look for available positions.

PUBLISHED JOB OPENINGS

You can find published job openings in a number of places, including your local paper (or the paper of the city to which you want or plan to move), career magazines, and other places. The problem with published job openings is that once published, the competition for that opening becomes more intense. Still, if you see a job opening that sounds interesting, submit your résumé. Just because it's not statistically the best way to find a job, some people do get jobs through advertisements published in newspapers, magazines, or other print publications.

One source of information about your local economy is your chamber of commerce. Ask for information about local companies, especially those that may be expanding or hiring.

WEB SITES

You can find a wealth of job-related sites on the Internet. Some provide job listings that you can search. Some provide job postings, where you can post your résumé; employers looking to fill positions can then search résumés and seek a match. Many provide career advice. Most provide a combination of these services.

The best and most well-known job site is Monster.com. This site enables you to search for jobs, network with its other members, and get career advice. To search for jobs, you must sign up for a monster account.

In addition to this site, you may also try some of the following:

◆ **Careerbuilder.com:** This site claims "900,000 jobs, The Internet's Largest Job Search & Employment site." You can search for jobs, post résumés, get advice, find resources, and obtain information about career fairs. The problem with this site (as well as others like it) is that "English" isn't really a job category. You can't choose English from the list and view related jobs. Instead, you have to browse through relevant categories (publishing, public relations, advertising, for example) or search for a particular job (editor, writer, and so on).

◆ **Collegegrad.com:** This site focuses on finding entr y-level jobs and includes help for preparing résumés, cover letters, interviews, and more.

◆ **Media Bistro** (www.mediabistro.com): This site lists editing jobs in the publishing world. You can search for online jobs, post your résumé, include highlights of y our wor k on the fr eelance page, read career advice articles, and more.

To find jobs related to writing or editing, search for "Writing Jobs" or "Editing Jobs" on a search engine such as Google and see what sites turn up. Try looking for sites that focus on a particular type of job. For example, you can find online job clubs or career sites dedicated to a particular field: The Write Jobs (www.writerswrite.com/jobs) is one example.

What can y ou gain fr om your Internet sear ch? Although y ou ar e hoping to find a job opening per fect for you, don't overlook the other information you can get from this search:

◆ Discover what are the hottest jobs. What are the most advertised jobs?

◆ Read the advice at the v arious sites to see ho w you can impr ove your chances of getting a job. Ignore, for the most par t, companies or advisors that make pr omises to improve your résumé and guarantee success *all* for one low payment of . . . . You don't have to pay for advice (unless y ou want to), especially on résumés or other common job-hunting topics such as interviewing.

◆ Look for companies or jobs of inter est. Although you may not get a particular job thr ough site postings, r eading through the types of jobs that ar e available and the companies that ar e hiring can help you pinpoint the exact position y ou seek. (You learn mor e about how to research different jobs in Chapter 6.)

NETWORKING

If the want ads and I nternet job sites often don 't wor k, what does? Networking. Most people find jobs thr ough word of mouth, thr ough networking, through asking around.

Chapter 3 talks about beginning to build a network while in school. Continue to do so in graduate school, during summer jobs, and with people you see socially. The more people included in your network, the better. Your network may include (but is not limited to):

- Family
- Friends
- Your family's friends
- Your friends' families
- Students
- Faculty
- Alumni
- Campus career center
- Former employers
- Former coworkers
- Customers or clients of former employers
- Competitors of former employers
- Neighbors

You can also network with any professionals you know, including your doctor, dentist, attorney, insurance agent, financial planner, hairdresser, barber, masseuse, personal trainer, coach, mechanic, veterinarian, bartender, child care provider, and more.

Tell each of these individuals specifically (not hinting or hemming and hawing around) that you are looking for a job. Give each a brief rundown on your education, your skills, and the type of job you want. For example, you might say "I recently graduated with a degree in English from Northwestern, and I am looking for a job in advertising, preferably an advertising assistant, but I'm eager to get started, so I'd be willing to consider other jobs in that field. I did an internship in media research, so I have the education and experience needed for this type of work." P rovide a résumé. Also, ask these contacts to pass along y   our information to any other people who may be able to help.

CAREER CENTER, ON-CAMPUS RECRUITERS, AND CAREER FAIRS

Your campus car eer center may sponsor car eer fairs or may host on-campus r ecruiters. (You can also find car eer fairs held thr ough other sources, such as your local paper.) These events are yet another possible source of job openings. Here's how to best take advantage of these events:

- ◆ **Find out who's going to attend.** If the fair, for example, is geared toward the medical field (a field that seems to always be in need of employees), you may decide to take a close look at the types of workers they seek. If they are basically looking for nurses or any-one in the nursing field and ther   e ar en't any oppor tunities for writing-related medical careers, skip the fair.

- ◆ **If the career fair is not limited to one area, take a look at the various companies that plan to attend.** Are there any compa-nies of interest to you? If so, make a list so that when you're at the fair, you can focus on these companies.

- ◆ **Dress for an interview (at least a casual interview).** Don't go in sweatpants and a T-shirt, even if you think you are just browsing through. I f someone wants to do an inter view on the spot, y ou should be dressed for the part—or at least close enough, given the casualness of the setting.

- ◆ **Prepare a short statement (some people call this the "elevator speech").** This should sum up y our education, experience, and career inter est. M emorize it so that y   ou get y our main points across, but make sur   e when y ou r ecite it, that y ou do so with enthusiasm and adding per tinent facts and details based on the situation. You don't want your statement to sound canned.

- ◆ **If you're asked what type of job you're seeking, be precise in explaining what you're looking for.** If the company is not hiring in that ar ea, ask the r epresentative if he or she kno   ws or can recommend someone who is in your area or is looking for someone with your skills. This representative may hold on to your résumé and pass it along if a colleague mentions that he's looking to hire someone.

♦ **If you do participate in an interview (or several), be sure to ask how the process works.** For example, if they ask for your résumé, does that mean they plan to call? Or are they just keeping it on file? If you do an initial interview, what's the next step? How should you follow up? When should you expect to hear from them? Don't walk away without knowing what is supposed to happen next.

FIND YOUR OWN JOB OPENINGS

Often, you identify in your career search a particular company or organization that you want to work for. You can approach such an organization directly to inquire about jobs. (You can also seek informational interviews, as discussed in Chapter 4, but remember that when you conduct an informational interview, you never ask for a job; you simply gather information.) Check the company's Web site for openings or talk to human resources about current and upcoming positions.

If you know you want to work for a particular company or industry, you can take an entry-level position at a company just to get your start. After you're hired, you'll gain the advantage of getting experience at the company. Plus, as mentioned, many jobs aren't advertised but are simply filled from within. Once you are "inside," you can keep alert to any possible new job positions and be first in line for consideration—sometimes even before the job has formally been posted.

Sometimes, the job you want hasn't been created. And although you may have a hard time getting people to listen to you so that you can sell them on the job, it can be done. This strategy works best if you're already working for your ideal company. You can then spot the need for this job, create your job description based on this need and your desires, and then "sell" the position to the company. You'll have more success if you show employers how the new job solves a problem, improves a situation, adds r evenue, or pr ovides some tangible benefit for the company or organization.

In trying to cr eate your own job, look for economic, business, and demographic trends. For example, the baby boomers are nearing retirement. Around 77 million Americans will start hitting retirement age in 2010. What does that mean for y ou as an E nglish major? What markets, jobs, needs might these people have for someone with your skills? This population of people will need estate planning, mental health care dealing with aging, help with insurance programs, activity programs for seniors, and advocates for issues relating to their population, just to name a few needs. Consider what need you can fulfill by creating a specific job or by looking for an existing job in this mar ket. Look for other demographic or economic trends and the opportunities they may present.

Interviewing for a Job

When y ou are asked for an inter view, don't expect to simply put on your newly shined shoes and be ready. You have some preparation work to do. You need to r esearch the company and organization.   You also need to practice for the inter view, anticipating the types of questions you'll be asked and preparing great responses. You then need to master a few interview tips and tricks. Finally, you need to know how to follow up after the interview. This section discusses these skills.

Do Your Research

Before the inter view, research the par ticular company or organization to find out more about it. What products does it make? What services does it offer? Who's the pr esident of the company/organization? I s it a public or   private company? H ow many people does the company employ? Where ar e the company headquar ters located? You should know the answers to these and other key questions about the company or organization.

To find this information, visit the company or organization 's Web site. M ost companies include a page " about us" or something similar that discusses the company 's histor y, mission statement, and so on. Look also for pages that describe how the company is organized, as well as who holds key positions. (Make note of these names.)

In addition, search the Internet for news stories about the company. Have they been in the news recently? If so, why? Are they launching a new product? cutting back? Have they won any awards? Try to make sure you're up to date on any current news relating to the company.

You may also consider visiting sites that provide company overviews, such as www .hoovers.com and www .vault.com. These sites include profiles of thousands of companies and include more detailed research about the specific company. For the most part, you can look up general information about the company at these sites. For complete, detailed information, you may need to be a subscriber (and pay a fee). Check with your school; it may have e accounts with these types of sites. You may also be able to get the detailed information by going through your school's career center's connection.

As another source, if you know someone who works or has worked for that company, you may want to talk to that person. He or she may give you a better sense of the company atmosphere as well as what employers at the company look for in potential employees.

PRACTICE

In addition to doing your research, prepare for the interview. In general, plan for five key points you want to make in the interview. Keep these points in mind; these are what you want the interviewer to remember about you. Also, be prepared to answer these typical questions:

- ◆ What do you know about our company? (Here's where that research pays off.)
- ◆ Tell me about yourself.
- ◆ What are your strengths/weaknesses?
- ◆ What would you like to change about yourself?
- ◆ Why did you leave your last job?
- ◆ Where do you see yourself five years from now?
- ◆ What are your goals?
- ◆ Why should I hire you?

In general, focus on what you can do for the company, not what the company can do for you. Tell the interviewer what makes you unique as a person, what special skills you have, and what distinguishes you from the other people who want this same job . Stress the preparation work you've done (see Chapter 3) and the experiences and skills y ou already have for this position.

SHINE IN THE INTERVIEW

In addition to being prepared for the questions, keep in mind the following interview tips:

- **Dress appropriately.** If you've visited the company, perhaps on an informational interview (see Chapter 3), you should get a sense of how employees dress. If you haven't visited, dress professionally— for example, a suit and tie for men and a suit, dr   ess, or other office-type outfit for women. Kno w the night before what you're going to w ear and make sur e it's ready—no tr ying to find hose without a run in them or pants that aren't missing a button at the last minute.

- **Be on time.** No excuses.

- **Use a firm handshake and be sure to remember the person's name.** Say the person 's name after y ou meet him ("I t's great to meet you, Bob"); this can help y ou remember the person's name. If the inter viewer has a car d, y ou may ask for one and keep it within sight. A t this time, y ou can also pr ovide another copy of your résumé (and business card, if you have one).

- **When asking a question, be precise and to the point.** Don't blab on and on. E mphasize y our str engths and sho w ho w y our experience or education makes you a good fit for the position.

- **Be friendly, but stick to professional issues.** Other topics, such as an acquaintance y ou have in common or an upcoming ev ent, may pop up. That's fine, but keep y our conversation focused on the job. Remember this is an interview, not a chat with a potential buddy.

FOLLOW UP

At the end of the interview, the interviewer may ask, "Do you have any questions?" You should hav e some questions pr epared, but don 't ask any old question just to ask a question. Above all else, don't ask, "Well, do I get the job?"

Instead, ask questions to learn mor e about the emplo yer and company. For example, you might ask how that person got his or her star t. Ask for additional information about the position, what exactly will you be doing, and with whom will y ou be working, for example. Also, try to get a sense of wher e the company is in the hiring pr ocess. Are there mor e people to inter view? H ow soon will a decision be made? When will the new employee be asked to start work?

It's key that you know what to do next and how the overall interview process works. For example, is this just an initial inter view and should you expect to be invited back at least two mor e times to talk to the department head and then human r esources before a hiring decision is made? With this information, you understand how the decision process happens.

Also make sur e y ou know what to do next. S hould y ou call back? Will you be called? If so, by what date? If the company hasn't called by that date, ask whether it's okay for you to follow up. Interviewing takes patience, but there's no sense waiting for a call if it's not going to come, so it 's per fectly reasonable to ask whether y ou can call after a cer tain time limit to check on the job progress.

Be sur e y ou send a handwritten thank-y ou note immediately after the inter view. Little touches such as this make a differ ence; y ou may find handwritten notes antiquated in the age of e-mail, but taking the time to write a note like this can make a big impr ession. Don't just say thank you in the note; restate your interest in the job as well as some of the reasons you think you are the perfect match for the position. (Even if you don't want the job after the interview, still send a thank-you note, but skip the parts about how you're a perfect match.)

If y ou don't get the job , try to learn mor e information about what you could have done differently. Don't be a pest about getting informa-tion and don't demand information—the company does not owe you a long (or any!) explanation. B ut if y ou have a means to do so, find out whether the job was filled by someone else and what that person's qualifications were. If no one was hired, was the position dropped?

Use any information you gain during the follow-up to evaluate your interview skills. Did someone more qualified get the position? Not too much you can do about that ex cept look for oppor tunities to incr ease your experience. D id someone y ou consider equal to y ou get the job? Perhaps he or she did a better job in the interview. What might you do better next time? Use each experience to better pr epare yourself for your next chance. Also, be sur e to ask the potential emplo yer to pass along your résumé to others looking to fill similar positions.

Chapter 6

Career Possibilities for an English Major

E nglish is not a vocational major that prepares you for one particular job (like an accountant, for example). Instead, a degree in English provides you with a broad range of skills useful for any number of careers. Skills that make you a good job candidate include the ability to:

- ◆ Think critically and solve problems

- ◆ Write and speak effectively

- ◆ Edit someone else's writing

- ◆ Express your creativity in any number of ways (design a brochure, write a campaign letter, reorganize an office, and others)

- ◆ Learn new information quickly

- ◆ Work well with others

- ◆ Develop hypotheses, research data, and interpret and summarize data

- ◆ Organize ideas and information

With these skills, English majors have achieved success in a variety of fields, including writing, editing, publishing, teaching, public relations, technical writing, paralegal and legal, mar keting, consulting, business, government, museums, libraries, consulting, and more.

This chapter takes a look at the v ariety of car eer possibilities av ailable to E nglish majors. Each section explains the r equirements, outlook, and salary range for this career path. Because you can do so much with a degr ee in E nglish (and this chapter couldn't cover all the possibilities in detail), the last section describes how to investigate other jobs relating to English (or careers that require skills related to English studies). There, you can explor e even more potential jobs, as w ell as learn how and where to research more detailed information.

Writers and Editors

Many people go into English with the goal of becoming a writer or editor; these car eers ar e pr obably most often associated with an E nglish degree. P ublishing and editing do pr   ovide many oppor tunities for work. This section takes a look at writing and editing opportunities.

WRITERS

A pr ofessional writer may wor k for any of the follo wing publications or organizations: ne wspapers, magazines, br oadcast media, trade and professional publications, consumer publications, adv ertising agencies, government agencies, colleges and univ   ersities, not-for-pr ofits, and businesses. Some writers are self-employed; their career is based on freelance writing jobs or assignments with one or mor   e publishers, and they may write essays, columns, opinion pieces, magazine articles, biographies, book reviews, and other pieces for publication.

Most creative writers, for example, are freelance writers and are self-employed. For this type of writing, the writer cr   eates original fiction and nonfiction texts for books, magazines, trade journals, ne wspapers, newsletters, radio and TV, and advertisements. If you want to be a creative writer, you might write shor t stories, no vels, poems, song lyrics, plays, screenplays, essays, columns, or other wor k for publication. You may be commissioned to write these wor ks (know in advance that the work will be published), or y ou may write the wor k and then seek to have it published.

Freelance writers usually have a good deal of writing experience that they got working for publications or companies. So although it's not a career you may be able to pursue immediately , it is one that y ou can aim and work toward as you gain more and more writing experience.

As another possibility, you may find wor k as a technical writer . In fact, this field pr ovides many new opportunities for writing. The next section discusses this type of writing in more detail.

TECHNICAL WRITERS

As mentioned, the best oppor tunities for a writing car eer are in technology. Technology is becoming incr easingly more complex and mor e prevalent. Also, ne w information and pr oducts ar e constantly being introduced. These factors cr eate a demand for technical writers who can teach people about products and how to use them or who can take complex information (scientific or medical information, for example) and convey it to a lay audience.

As a technical writer , you may r esearch and write about pr oducts. Types of publications y ou might cr eate include user manuals, catalogs and par ts lists, training materials, mar keting information, and so on. You might also write pr oposals r equesting funds and facilities for research. The median salary for entry-level technical writers is $41,000.

If you want to pursue a car eer in this ar ena, you need a degr ee plus some specialized technical knowledge depending on the field in which you want to wor k. For example, y ou might specializ e in science, law , medicine, engineering, business, or computers by taking classes in these subjects, getting a minor in these fields, or pursuing r elevant wor k experience.

EDITORS

In addition to pursuing a writing car eer, some English majors look for work as an editor. Editors, according to the 2002 Occupation Outlook Handbook, hold 130,000 jobs. I n the technology field, technical editors account for 50,000 jobs.

Editors work for ne wspapers, magazines, book publishers, business and not-for-profit organizations, adv ertising agencies, public r elations firms, radio and TV stations, and go vernment agencies. S ome small and many large companies have in-house newsletters and other materials that require an editor or writer.

What do editors do? To start, they assess the needs of their particular audience and then plan and cr eate publications based on these needs. They may use in-house writers or hir e outside writers and negotiate contracts. Or if the publication has a writing staff (for example, a newspaper or magazine), the editor may assign articles or assignments. Once the work is received, the editor reviews, edits, checks facts, and rewrites, as needed. F inally, the editor may o versee the pr oduction of the final product (book, magazine issue, newspaper, and so on).

An English major is a good fit for a career as an editor. If you want to pursue newspaper or magazine editing, you may also consider getting a certificate or minor in journalism. For all editing work, seek out experiences (campus activities, internships, and part-time jobs—see Chapter 3) working as a writer or editor.

ENTRY-LEVEL JOBS

Most editors hav e assistants, and this is a good entr y-level job to gain experience in this field. For example, an editorial assistant may evaluate manuscripts, format text, and help coor dinate photography, illustrations, and graphics. B ut then again, an editorial assistant may make photocopies, pr epare packages to ship out, and do that sor t of gr unt work. Still, you may be able to get y our start in this position, wor king for a book publisher or other kind of publisher (magazine, newspaper).

WRITING AND EDITING OUTLOOK

You can get curr ent information on the number of jobs and outlook for writing and editing fr om the *Bureau of Labor Statistics Occupation Outlook Handbook.* The most r ecent edition notes that writers and editors held 319,000 jobs in 2002. M ore than one-thir d w ere self-employed, and mor e than one-half wor ked in the information sector (newspaper, periodical, book, and directory publishers, motion picture and sound recording industries, Internet Service Providers, Web search portals, data pr ocessing ser vices, and I nternet publishing). The next biggest categor y of writers wor ked in adv ertising and r elated fields; these writers account for 139,000 jobs.

The handbook says that job oppor   tunities ar e expected to gr ow about as fast as the av erage for all occupations thr ough 2012. Because more companies ar e adding ne wsletters and/or Web sites and because information is becoming mor e and mor e specialized, the demand for writers and editors should incr ease, especially for writers with   Web experience

Most writers work a 40-hour week, but may also have to work over-time to meet publication deadlines. Also, if y ou want to wor k for a major publisher or advertising agency, you may need to relocate. Many of the jobs are concentrated in big cities where major publishers and ad agencies are located. New York, Chicago, L.A., Boston, and Philadelphia are the most common places for publishing and advertising careers.

SALARY INFORMATION

The follo wing table pr ovides median and high and lo w salar y infor-mation for writing and editing car eers. This information is based on the most curr ent statistics fr om the B ureau of Labor and S tatistics (www.bls.gov).

Job	Median	Lowest 10% Range	Highest 10% Range
Salaried writers and authors	$42,790	> $21,320	< $85,140
Salaried technical writers	$50,580	> $30,270	< $80,900
Editors	$41,170	> $24,010	< $76,620

Journalism Careers

If you enjoy writing, y ou may purse a journalism car eer, wor king as a news analyst, r eporter, or corr espondent. These pr ofessionals gather information, and then write stories or articles for publication. For radio or TV, ne ws analysts (also called ne wscasters or ne ws anchors) collect information from various sources and then br oadcast the stor y on the radio or TV (either liv e or thr ough a videotape). O ften, news analysts specialize in a particular news area, such as sports, weather, investigative reporting, and so on.

Reporters look into breaking news stories that affect the local, state, national, or international scene. B y following up on tips, inter viewing witnesses or participants, taking pictures, and visiting sites, they organize the facts into a coherent story and then write an article for a written publication or air their reports on the radio or TV. Some reporters have a specific ar ea (or beat) that they co   ver, including health, politics, sports, entertainment, science, business, technology, and others.

News and Reporters Job Outlook

News correspondents report on news from their location (big cities or international sites). N ews r eporters and corr espondents held 66,000 jobs in 2002. M ost of these people (60 per cent) work for newspapers, periodical, book, and dir ectory publishers. A bout 25 per cent work in radio and TV broadcasting, and 4,100 w ere self-employed. Because of mergers, the closing of many ne   ws organizations, and competition from cable TV, the field is highly competitiv e. Overall, job opportunities are moving at a pace slower than the average. Because the media are supported by advertising, the job outlook is also affected b y economic fluctuations. For example, when the economy is down (and advertising agencies aren't placing ads), the job outlook reflects this.

Working conditions for a journalism car eer can be str essful. Often, this type of wor k r equires trav el, as w ell as being on call to handle breaking news. Working hours vary and don't follow the traditional 9-to-5 schedule. F or example, some   TV stations br oadcast ne ws 24/7, and the reporting staff needs to be available at all hours and work long hours. Newspaper deadlines are often late at night. Meeting these deadlines also adds to the stress factor.

Although most employers in this field prefer a degree in journalism, English majors may also be consider ed for these jobs. I n addition to English, you may consider taking journalism classes, getting a minor in journalism, or getting a journalism cer tificate. For TV and radio, consider specializing in broadcast journalism. As a student, look for practical experience wor king on a school ne wspaper, magazine, Web site, or other publication. Also, consider internships or summer jobs wor king for a news organization.

SALARY INFORMATION FOR REPORTERS AND OTHER JOURNALISTS

Salaries vary widely. You can get some idea of the range of salaries b y reviewing the follo wing statistics fr om the B ureau of Labor and Statistics site:

◆ The median salar y for ne ws analysts, r eporters, and corr espondents was $30,510 in 2002.

◆ The lowest 10 percent earned less than $17,620.

◆ The highest 10 percent earned more than $69,450.

◆ For radio and TV, the median salary was $33,320.

◆ For ne wspaper, magazines, books, and dir ectories, the median was $29,090.

Advertising and Public Relations

Two other fields wor th inv estigating ar e adv ertising and public r elations. Like other careers covered in this chapter, advertising and public relations both require good writing and communication skills. This section pr ovides a r eview of some r elevant car eer oppor tunities in these areas, including a public relations specialist and advertising copywriter.

PUBLIC RELATIONS SPECIALIST

As a public relations specialist, you prepare and distribute information about y our clients to the media, often in the form of pr ess r eleases. Many businesses, not-for-pr ofit organizations, univ ersities, hospitals, government agencies, and other organizations hire public relations staff to manage their image. The public r elations specialist pr omotes noteworthy ev ents and keeps the public informed about an organization 's policies, activities, and accomplishments. F or example, a public r elations specialist (or press secretary) who works for a government agency keeps the public up to date on go vernment pr ograms, issucs, legislation, campaigns, and news.

Public relations specialists hav e contacts in the media and collabo-
rate with the pr ess, pr oviding them with information on stories or
events. PR staff also plan conv entions, host community events such as
speakers, pr epare comments or speeches for company or go vernment
officials, pr epare annual r eports for in-house use as w ell as for the
public, make pr esentations, create training manuals and policies-and-
procedures handbooks, and write proposals.

Most employers require a degree or advanced degree in journalism or
public relations, although someone with an E nglish degree and ex cel-
lent writing skills can also succeed in this field. K ey criteria for getting
a job in public relations include a relevant internship or summer work,
as well as a portfolio of published work. For example, you may work for
your school's alumni association, publishing stories for the ne wsletter
or writing press releases for the local media.

Like journalists, public r elations specialists often hav e to be on call
in case of breaking news stories, emergencies, or other crisis. The typical work day is usually not 9 to 5. F or example, a public r elations specialist may need to attend community meetings in the ev   ening or
special events held on weekends. Travel may also be required.

As for the outlook, public r elations specialists held about 158,000
jobs in 2002, most concentrated in ser vice industries such as adv ertising, health care, social assistance, educational services, and government.
Other employers included communication firms and financial organizations. About 11,000 public relations specialists are self-employed.

Salary information breaks down as follows:

- The median salary for public relations specialists was $41,170 in
  2002.

- The lowest 10 percent earned less than $24,240.

- The highest 10 percent earned more than $75,100.

- Public relations specialists who worked in advertising or a related
  field had the highest median salar y: $48,070. This was follo wed
  by government ($42,000); business, pr ofessional, labor, political,
  or similar organizations ($39,330); and colleges, universities, and
  professional schools ($36,820).

ADVERTISING COPYWRITER

In addition to public relations, advertising is another area that provides opportunities for E nglish majors. The skills of writing and speaking effectively, as well as the ability to integrate images, are key.

You may consider any number of careers within advertising. Usually, you start with an entry-level job, possibly as an assistant or adv ertising copywriter. As you gain experience, y ou may advance to other car eers, including advertising or promotion manager or marketing manager.

An advertising copywriter creates ads for radio and TV to promote the sale of goods or ser vices. In this job, the copywriter star ts by consulting with sales media and mar keting representatives to learn about the product or service. Collectively, this group may brainstorm to come up with ideas about a particular advertisement or campaign. For example, they may think about the style, format, medium for the ad, and other factors.

The copywriter then writes, edits, and pr oofreads the text for the advertisement and may also make suggestions for the art, photographs, or illustrations to be included. The copywriter might also help estimate production costs, o versee work done b y outside contractors, and pr e-pare a marketing program. In addition to writing the ads, a copywriter needs to keep current on trends in advertising and consumer buying.

Advertising copywriters wor k for adv ertising agencies, adv ertisers (department stores), the media (radio, TV, cable, newspapers, and mag-azines), public r elations firms, and trade organizations. M any jobs ar e located in cities that hav e major ad agencies, most notably N ew York, but also Chicago and Los Angeles.

Beginning salaries are usually under $30,000, but the salary increases as you advance in the field. For example, the median income for adver-tising and promotions managers was $57,130.

Teaching

Another career path for English majors is teaching. As an elementary or secondary school teacher , y ou pr epare lesson plans and instr uct children or adolescents and ev aluate their per formance. P ublic schools require state certification as well as a college degree with specific education courses and a semester internship. Private schools require a college degree, but may or may not require certification by the state.

For a high school job , you may also need to hav e some kno wledge and experience in the par ticular subject(s) y ou will be teaching. F or example, if y ou want to teach high school E nglish, you can major in English literatur e or E nglish education. S ome E nglish pr ograms include teaching certification as part of the program.

A bachelor's degr ee may be enough to star t with, but the state or school district will ev entually want y ou to wor k to ward a master 's degree. The school district may help y ou do y our graduate wor k or complete other training you'll need for certification. For example, your school district may offer tuition subsidies, flexible scheduling, and other forms of practical assistance. N ote also that a master 's degr ee is required to teach at the college lev el, and a doctorate degr ee is usually required for fulltime professorships at the university level.

Preschool, kindergar ten, elementar y, middle, and secondar y school teachers held about 3.8 million jobs in 2002. About 90 percent worked for public school systems; 10 per cent worked for priv ate schools. The numbers broke down by school as follows:

School	Number of Teachers
Elementary	1.5 million
Secondary	1.1 million
Middle	602,000
Preschool	424,000
Kindergarten	168,000

The demand for teachers is expected to gr ow, as curr ent teachers retire and as public inter est in education rises. Also, oppor tunities will vary depending on location and subject.

Salaries vary widely by locale, but usually begin in the mid-$30,000 range. The median salary ranged from $39,810 to $44,340 for all pr e-school to secondar y school teachers. The bottom 10 per cent earned between $24,960 and $29,850; the top 10 per   cent earned betw een $62,890 and $68,530.

Teachers' aides, who help classroom teachers prepare and teach lessons and evaluate students' progress, do not face the same certification requirements (although a background check is usually required). Salaries for teacher aides are $19,000 to $23,000 per year.

Librarians

Librarians ar e emplo yed b y schools, univ ersities, corporations, and public libraries. English majors may find entr y-level jobs as a librarian aide or, if y ou pursue a master 's of librar y science degr ee (MLS), y ou may work as a librarian.

In the past, librarians dealt with mostly print resources, but with the explosion of the Internet and other technology, more and more librarians use these sour ces to r esearch and classify information.   They also help patrons and students find the information they need.

In addition to user services (helping patrons and students find information), librarians also deal with technical ser vices, including acquiring, cataloging, and pr eparing new materials for use.   They may cr eate lists of books, periodicals, articles; coordinate special programs, such as storytelling for kids; negotiate contracts for ser   vices and equipment; help promote the library through public relations, fundraising, or other efforts; review new books and catalogs to keep up to date on ne w publications; and more.

Librarians ar e emplo yed b y public and school libraries as w   ell as libraries maintained b y go vernment agencies, corporations, law firms, ad agencies, r eligious organizations, museums, pr ofessional associates, medical centers, and research facilities.

In 2002, librarians held roughly 167,000 jobs, with nearly one-third working for public libraries, and the job demand is expected to gr ow. (Many librarians are expected to retire in the next ten years.)

Salaries vary depending on the type, size, and location of the library. The median salary was $43,090 in 2002. The lowest 10 percent earned less than $24,510; the highest 10 percent earned more than $66,590.

Still More Career Possibilities

This chapter touches on only a few of the many career possibilities for a student with a degree in English. But don't be limited to these suggestions. Think about your skills. Employers aren't looking for the content knowledge, but rather for the skills and characteristics y ou have (creativity, computer skills, research skills, and so on).

This section provides a list of some other job ideas to consider You'll also learn ho w to find out mor e about these (or any jobs) as w ell as where to look for other jobs recommended for English majors.

JOBS FOR ENGLISH MAJORS

Most colleges pr ovide a list or information on their   Web site with examples of the types of car eers applicable to a major in E nglish. For example, The University of Texas (www.utexas.edu/student/careercenter/careers) lists applicable careers for specific majors.

Top Jobs for Women

What are the top-paying professions for women with an undergraduate degree according to a recent "On the Job" column in *All Woman?* They are:

Job	Salary ($)
Pharmacist	74,900
Computer software engineer	73,200
Computer programmer	60,100
Financial services sales agent	59,700
Personal financial adviser	57,700
Market research analyst	53,400
Registered nurse	46,700
Accountant	45,400
Writer	42,500
Public relations specialist	41,000

You can find other similar lists at the following:

- University of North Carolina's "What Can I Do With a Major In . . .?" (www.uncw.edu/stuaff/career/majors)

- University of Kansas Academic Majors Career Resources (www.ukans.edu/~uces/major/index.shtml)

- Florida State University's Match Major Sheets (career.fsu.edu/ccis/matchmajor/matchmenu.html)

- University of Tennessee's "What Can I do with this degree?" (career.utk.edu/majors/majors.asp)

RESEARCHING CAREER PARTICULARS

If you find a career of interest and want to find more detailed information (job description, salary range, work environment, requirements, likely employers, professional associations, and other useful information), you can use any number of resources to locate this information. Some popular resources include:

- **The Occupational Outlook Handbook:** Hard copy in library or online at www.bls.gov/oco.

- **O*NETL:** Includes more comprehensive information about careers and outlooks (online.onetcenter.org)

AND THE LIST GOES ON . . .

Nothing seem a fit yet? Then review the following list of other career possibilities:

- Account executive
- Actor/actress
- Analyst
- Artist
- Bank officer

- Biographer
- Book critic
- Bookstore manager
- Business manager
- Circulation assistant
- City manager
- Columnist
- Comedian
- Comedy writer
- Communications manager
- Congressional aide
- Crossword puzzle writer
- Curator
- Curriculum planner
- Desktop publisher
- Director
- Documentation specialist
- Editor, film/video
- Editorial assistant
- Educational program specialist
- Entertainment agent
- ESL teacher
- Fact checker
- Fashion merchandiser
- Fundraiser
- Greeting card writer

- Hotel manager
- Human resources corporate communication
- Human resources trainer
- Insurance agent
- Interpreter and translator
- Lawyer
- Legal assistant
- Literary agent
- Lobbyist
- Magazine writer
- Manuscript reader
- Market research
- Media planner
- Narrator
- Novelist
- Paralegal
- Personnel manager
- Playwright
- Poet
- Politician
- Pollster
- Product manager
- Proofreader
- Public information specialist
- Publicity assistant
- Research assistant

- Sales representative
- Script reader
- Singer
- Special events coordinator
- Speech writer
- Sports writer
- Technical consultant
- Travel writer
- Video scriptwriter/producer
- Web content manager
- Web developer

Chapter 7

Case Studies

The best way to learn about how to find a job and the various types of ways you can use an English degree is to listen to and read about real stories, real people, and real experiences. That's the focus of this chapter: case studies that focus on several different individuals. From each story, you can see how that person found the job, what he or she likes about it, as how you an succeed in a similar job. From these case studies, you gain insight into the many possibilities available to English majors and learn how to take steps in your own educational and career quest.

In this chapter, you read about a variety of people with a variety of jobs from a librarian to a speech writer. Although the careers and career paths vary, they all share one thing in common: They majored in English.

Michele, a College Librarian

If you want to be a librarian, there are many jobs available: archivist, rare book dealer, database administrator, conservator, records manager, information architect, and others. Librarians specialize in all sorts of areas, including law, music, business, children's services, public policy, medicine, and others. This section focuses on Michele, a librarian at a small college.

WHY I MAJORED IN ENGLISH

When I was little, my mom sometimes took my books away to encourage me to play outside to play That's how much I loved to read. My 4th and 5th grade teacher (the same teacher for both years) encouraged my love of books and r eading. Through her involvement with a children's literature program, she was introduced to new authors, and she brought these authors into our classr oom. It was thrilling to meet the actual authors who made up these wonderful stories.

When I went to college, I star ted to think about a major in E nglish because of this long standing inter est in literatur e and r eading. I also considered American histor y because, like E nglish, it was a subject in which I was interested and I enjoyed many of the classes taught by great professors in my first y ear or so at college. B ecause I did not want to double major in both E nglish and histor y, I had to choose one for my major and one for my minor I ended up choosing my major by a flip of the coin!

During college, I wor ked in the campus librar y my fr eshman year, and then I wor ked at the alumnae magazine for my last thr ee years of college. I thought I would get inv olved in publishing after graduation, and my first entr y-level job was in publishing, but it did not pay w ell. So after a y ear, I held a v ariety of office jobs. I was wor king as a legal secretary when I decided to go back to school for my librar y degr ee. People who know me have always said that I should become a librarian!

I ended up becoming a college librarian at a small, specializ ed college. In this work, I provide reference help, teach bibliographic instruction classes, catalog librar y acquisitions, or der interlibrar y loans, maintain the server and library OPAC (Online Public Access Catalog), manage the College ar chives, serve on academic committees, academically advise students, and sometimes cover the circulation desk.

HOW MY ENGLISH MAJOR PREPARED ME FOR MY JOB

My major in English taught me how to write as well as how to research. I also learned ho w to find the underlying meaning fr om the written word—that is, what the author meant but did not explicitly say . This skill now helps me at the reference desk: I can better understand what a library patron wants from the information that he or she requests.

WHAT OTHER TRAINING I RECEIVED

If you have just an undergraduate degree, you can find some entry-level clerical positions at a librar y. If y ou want to be a librarian, though, you need a master's degr ee in librar y science, either an MLS (master o library science) or a MLIS (master of librar y and information science). The American Librar y Association accr edits librar y schools in the United States. As with other degrees, a diploma from an accredited institution is more highly regarded than a diploma fr om a nonaccredited institution.

I got the MLIS, which is the ne wer version of the degr ee, from an accredited school. This degr ee co vers the larger r ole computers no w play in the library. I did the MLIS full-time for two years. Then I stayed on for another semester to do additional specialization in P reservation Administration. I did not complete my Ph.D.

Like many students in the program, I worked 20 hours a week at one of the libraries on campus, and I also completed an internship during my last semester . M any of my classes r equired practical pr ojects that placed me in r eal libraries and ar chives. From these classes, super vised by the instructor and an experienced librarian in the collection, I both learned about the subject and did actual professional work.

Currently librarians are not required to get licensed or certified (like a teacher). You do need the teaching license if you want to work in elementary and secondary school libraries. If you plan to teach library and information science at the college lev el, y ou usually need a P h.D. in library science. Also, some positions require a second master's degree or a Ph.D. in another field. For example, law librarians usually have a law degree in addition to the library school degree.

WHAT HELPED ME SUCCEED

Before going back to school to pursue my master's degree in library science, I spoke with several professional librarians in a variety of settings and I shadowed one of them for a day. This gave me an overview of the profession and confirmed my inter est in this car eer path. M y internships and practical class work also helped me achieve success.

The one r egret that I hav e is that I wish that I would hav e gone to library school a couple of y ears earlier than I did. I fought ev eryone's expectations of me (that I should be a librarian), ev   en though they were right.

How I Landed This Job

I wound up at my present job because of the tech bust. Many librarians went to wor k in technology companies, especially star tups, in S ilicon Valley during the boom y ears, and many of them (like me) lost their jobs when everyone went out of business. Other private employers were laying-off workers, especially in " nonessential" areas like r ecords man-agement or information specialist. Library jobs also became fairly scarce as many public systems cut jobs or at fr   oze hiring for " nonessential" positions because their budgets w   ere cut b y local and state go   vern-ments. All these factors added up to a lot of competition for the jobs that were available.

I found the listing for this position on a local library association Web site and r ealized that I had the r   equired qualifications because of the preprofessional wor k experience that I picked up while in graduate school, plus the versatility of certain skill sets like customer service and the organization of information. To get the job, I repositioned my skills and knowledge within this ne w context and sold these skills thr   ough the cover letter and interview process.

Librarianship is a huge field, and the MLIS degr ee is very versatile. I've also worked as a database manager at a high-tech star tup company in Silicon Valley, in public libraries, and on a bookmobile. F riends of mine in the librar y field hold librar y-related jobs in law firms, busi-nesses, government agencies, and private special collections.

The Good and Bad about My Work

As for the positive aspects of my job, I love the variety. I get to help with the fun par t of r esearch pr ojects—finding information—and get to leave the actual writing of the paper to the students. I like interacting with students and faculty, especially when they are excited about a par-ticular topic. I also enjoy sorting through materials in the ar chives and learning about the histor y of the school and the individuals who attended and worked here.

On the downside, I dislike meetings. Sometimes they are a waste of time and energy. Also, an academic librarian must deal with the politics of academia. The academic world can be very different from the business world. Faculty can be very idealistic and opinionated; they also often do not understand the bottom line. On the other hand, academia is a place of free expression, and creativity is encouraged.

MY WORK AND MY LIFE

I typically work 40 hours per week, 52 weeks a year with vacation and sick leave. A more typical academic librarian is on a 9- or 10-month contract with an unpaid summer vacation.

I belong to several professional associations, including The American Library Association (ALA) and the California Library Association (CLA). The ALA, the national association, deals with the whole field of librarianship. Most states have their own association; these work with the ALA but concentrate on more regional issues like state spending and legislation. You can also find many more specialized associations that focus on specific areas within the field. For example, there is the Public Libraries Association, the Society of American Archivists, the Special Libraries Association, the Association of Research Libraries, the Medical Library Association, the Music Library Association, and many others.

Christine, a Lawyer

Another career possibility for English majors is to pursue a law degree after completing an undergraduate degree. This case study is based on Christine, a lawyer who specializes in real estate and usually handles private residential contracts.

WHY I MAJORED IN ENGLISH

I've always liked to read, and I had a great professor for freshman English, so I signed up to take another course with him. One thing led to another, and I was halfway to an English major, so I just went with it. I had no idea what I would do with it, but I enjoyed the classes and read a lot of great books.

How My English Major Prepared Me for My Job

The analytical writing skills I had to learn when I was studying English literature are invaluable to me now as a lawyer. Learning to state my position clearly and supporting my arguments are critical skills for me as a lawyer.

What Other Training I Received

After completing my degree in English, I decided to pursue a law degree, and the first part of that process was getting accepted to law school. For this, I had to take the LSAT, submit applications to the law schools I considered attending, and set up interviews and letters of recommendation. Personally, I didn't find the LSAT so difficult. I did take some practice tests to familiarize myself with the different types of questions on the LSAT.

I completed my law degree, and the next step was to pass the bar exam. The bar exam was the hardest part. I'd heard so many horror stories, and I knew people who had to retake it after failing the first time. Fortunately, my law school recommended a great bar review course, and some of my classmates and I arranged a study group. These elements were critical to my success in passing the exam.

What Helped Me Succeed

The one thing throughout both my undergraduate and graduate degrees that helped me the most were study groups. Throughout high school and college, I always tried to start or join study groups. My bar exam course and study group were also key to my passing the bar. Study groups are a great way to not only prepare for exams but also bond with your classmates and make friends.

I think one of the challenges I faced was my motivation. I didn't have a lifelong goal of becoming a lawyer, and I didn't go into law out of some great passion for law and justice. In hindsight, I probably could have gone a lot farther a lot faster if I had settled on law as a career early on instead of just going with the flow.

THE GOOD AND BAD ABOUT MY WORK

The thing I love most about my job is this: I can make things happen for people. My clients are usually families about to move into a new home. Whether they're buying their first home or upgrading to their dream house, they're so excited. When I handle the legal matters for them and when the sale goes through smoothly, I'm part of that good feeling. I'm not exactly saving the world with my law degree, but it's a lot more meaningful to me than what I was doing before (working for a large corporation).

What I dislike most is the paper work. Even when there are secretaries and junior associates to help, dealing with the paperwork is a full-time job on its own. It doesn't help that everything is written in legalese, in which sentences are twice as wordy and half as understandable as in normal English.

I also don't love some of the formalities surrounding the practice of law. Sometimes, things could be streamlined, but they take twice as long because everything has to be done a certain way.

HOW I LANDED THIS JOB

When I first started out, I worked for a big corporate firm. The pay was good, but the hours were long. The long hours were particularly hard on me as a newlywed. My husband is a lawyer, too, so he understood, but it was still frustrating to have so little time together.

I left the corporate world when I went on maternity leave with my first child. Then I started working part-time at my husband's firm; he and his dad went into practice together. This is where I still work, and I like this arrangement much better. I like working out in the suburbs, closer to home, and in a much more relaxed environment. I can dress more casually, which is a big help to a working mother with two small children! And of course, it's great to be working with my husband, and I adore my father-in-law. Although I don't make the same kind of money as I did working for a big corporate law firm, the other benefits make my new job absolutely worth it.

Fran, a Journalist

Some English majors go on to become journalists, parlaying their writing abilities into a career in newspaper publishing, radio, TV, or magazines. This section looks at the case study of F ran, a journalist who works for a local tourism magazine. I n her wor k, Fran researches new developments in her city, checks out local resources, and stays on top of upcoming events.

WHY I MAJORED IN ENGLISH

I always loved literature and writing classes, and I always preferred essay questions on exams. I did better on r esearch papers than on parr oting back answers on tests. So when I star ted college, I decided to focus on English. I knew that English courses would require more of the things I was good at and less of the things I struggled with.

HOW MY ENGLISH MAJOR PREPARED ME FOR MY JOB

As a journalist, it's important to be well read and culturally knowledgeable. I had lots of experiences with r eading and cultur e from all those books I had to r ead as an E nglish major. Also, the emphasis on essay writing in E nglish was a big help . The English curriculum gav e me a strong gr ounding in organizing my thoughts and expr   essing ideas clearly and concisely, the way I have to when I write articles.

WHAT OTHER TRAINING I RECEIVED

Although I majored in English, I did also get a master's degree in journalism while I was wor king. My editors encouraged me to pursue this degree, and the magazine I wor k for was r eally accommodating of my schedule.

Even though I do hav e an adv anced degr ee, I still think the best training is on the job . J ust getting out ther e and writing ar ticles— starting with really simple announcements, paying attention to the editors' critiques—is the best experience for a journalist in training. If you want to be a journalist, seek out oppor tunities to get y our words and ideas into print. You may wor k for the college ne wspaper or magazine or your own local paper. As another idea, consider working on publications for organizations, clubs, associations, chur ch gr oups, not-for-profit organizations, businesses, and so on. E ven if you have to donate your time and effor t, the chance to actually hav e your work published really pays off.

WHAT HELPED ME SUCCEED

As mentioned, I think the best training is doing r   eal wor k. To that effect, I was always involved in on-campus journalism: the school newspaper, the yearbook, or whatever else was available. These opportunities gave me a lot of early experience in things like interviewing, prioritizing ideas, and dealing with deadlines.   The r elated skills and experiences also looked great on my résumé.

I also took advantage of the resources at the career center at my college, using these r esources, for example, to find summer jobs in journalism. In addition to the campus writing, my summer jobs allowed me to get a v ariety of experiences with differ ent kinds of publications and ultimately helped me to get a full-time job when I graduated. The job listings at the car eer center, in addition to helping me find jobs, also opened my eyes to a lot of the differ ent types of jobs in the field that I might not have known about.

THE GOOD (AND BAD) ABOUT MY JOB

I love the entrée my job giv es me into all sor ts of cultural ev ents and places in the city . Clubs can be ex clusive, concer ts and theater tickets can be hard to get, and restaurants can be expensive, but my press pass solves a lot of those pr oblems, and the magazine pays the bills. I ev en get into ev ents that most people don 't, like opening nights and back-stage parties. This is great stuff for someone who loves my city and all it has to offer. Another particularly nice perk is that I often get to bring a guest with me. I've taken dates out to dinner, treated friends to a show, and even brought my mother to a day spa.

As for the downside, well, no one loves deadlines. And I don't always enjoy all of my writing assignments. Although I love most of the places the magazine sends me, ther e hav e been a fe w I'd just as soon hav e skipped. Sometimes the music or the food is r eally bad or it just may not be my taste, but it's still my job to go there and write about it.

Also, although a tourism magazine is generally supposed to be upbeat, it also has to be informativ e. That means letting r eaders know about problems they may encounter. I've had to cover accidents, disasters, and ev en crimes that hav e an impact on visitors to the city , and those are upsetting. I've seen a fe w things that literally gav e me nightmares.

Finally, I prefer assignments that actually inv olve writing an ar ticle, but sometimes I get stuck writing up a calendar of events. I realize that's helpful to our r eaders, but wor king on it is r eally tedious. As I gain more experience and seniority at the magazine, I won 't have to do as much of this type of writing anymore.

MY WORK AND MY LIFE

A lot of my work takes place outside the office and often inv olves covering events that take place in the evening, so my job is not a traditional 9-to-5 situation. I have mandatory weekly staff meetings, and I have to attend and be on time for the ev ents I co ver, but for the most par t I make my o wn schedule. As long as I turn in my assigned stories on time, I don't have to arrive or leave at the same time every day or at the same time as everyone else.

I've met people who seem to find my wok hours suspect, like it's not really a full-time job or a serious job , especially because my job often seems to involve going to the latest hot spots. But I do work hard.

I like the flexibility of my schedule. I don't have to get the boss's permission to take time off to go to the dentist, and no one cares if I take a long lunch. I want to have a family of my own someday, and I think my job's flexibility would be a big adv antage. I f I had kids, I pr obably wouldn't want to co ver quite as many ev ening events, but my city has plenty of daytime things to cover, too.

Dan, a Political Speechwriter

If you're interested in politics, y ou may use y our English major to get involved in that ar ea. You might, for example, wor k on a campaign, creating letters, brochures, and other written publications for a particular candidate or cause. O ne English major combined his writing skills and lo ve of a cause to jump-star t a car eer as a political speechwriter . Dan, the subject of this case, writes speeches and cr eates ne wsletter material for a city council representative.

WHY I MAJORED IN ENGLISH

I'm a little embarrassed to admit it no w, but there were two main r easons why I major ed in English: poetry and my poetr y professor. I lo ve poetry. As a teenager, I used to write a lot of angst-y poems, so I signed up for a poetry course in college. I then promptly developed a crush on the professor, which is the other reason I majored in English.

HOW MY ENGLISH MAJOR PREPARED ME FOR MY JOB

English majors at my college must take a senior seminar, which means choosing a seminar that covers a genre of special instance. For example, students might explor e feminist literatur e, nineteenth-centur y no vels, or Jewish writing. I took this opportunity to combine my English skills with an issue that impor tant to me. I got inv olved with a student activist gr oup in college that dealt with this issue, and I then studied major writers' wor k on this issue.   When I ended up wor king for a politician, I not only had the writing skills fr om studying gr eat literature, but I also had some expertise on a topic of importance to him and his constituents, as well as to me.

WHAT OTHER TRAINING I RECEIVED

My job didn 't r equire any fur ther formal education, like a graduate degree or certification, although there was a security check. Most of my additional training was on the job.

HOW I LANDED THIS JOB

When I was in college, a few people from my student group—including me—volunteered to help a councilman who suppor ted our cause. A t first, I handled menial tasks, such as stuffing env elopes and things like that. Because a local election campaign doesn 't have a huge staff , the candidate got to kno w some of the v olunteers very well. As he got to know me, he star ted picking my brain for ideas about ho w to attract more y oung v oters. When he found out I was an E nglish major, he would say "Hey, Dan, you're an English major. What's another way of saying this?" E ventually, I star ted helping him edit and write his speeches. After he was elected and I graduated, he hired me to work for him full-time.

WHAT HELPED ME SUCCEED

Although I can't guarantee this will get ev eryone a job, I str ongly recommend studying things that interest you, getting involved in a worthwhile cause, and volunteering for something you believe in. Even if the candidate I volunteered for hadn't hired me, I met a number of people on the campaign trail who were also good contacts, and I still feel great about helping to get the right guy elected. Along the way I learned a lot of other impor tant things, like ho w to deal with many differ ent kinds of people and how to state a controversial position in a politically adept way, instead of ranting and raving.

THE GOOD AND BAD ABOUT MY WORK

I love working for an elected official who r epresents a cause that's near and dear to my heart. It's a great challenge and a great responsibility to know that I put the wor ds in his mouth that can persuade people to vote or legislate in ways that will affect people 's liv es. B eyond that, I love knowing that I'm responsible for some of the councilman's greatest lines, like the quotes that become sound bites on the evening news.

On the downside, there's a lot of infighting and backstabbing in politics. The councilman is a great guy, but I have to deal with a lot of difficult people who can make things difficult for me as w ell as for the councilman.

Also, my job can be v ery high pressure at times. To get it just right, speechwriting requires a lot of r evisions. For example, I might need to make last-minute changes if something happens in the news that needs to be addressed in the speech. The work is challenging and exciting, but also kind of nerve-wracking!

MY WORK AND MY LIFE

Theoretically, I work normal business hours, but in reality, my schedule is very different from 9 to 5. Some days, I have to work late with the staff to get a newsletter or other publication out. Sometimes, the boss wants some of the staff to come with him to an event or appearance. Just like his personal assistant is there to handle all those little details like taking his coat and making sure the transportation is arranged, I have to be ready to tweak his speeches, especially if something happens during the course of the evening that he feels he needs to address. If there's some breaking news that we need to react to, I might even get a phone call in the middle of the night. Fortunately, that hasn't happened very often!

As another example, I work late when the mayor makes the annual state-of-the-city address. The councilman, staff, and I watch this together. I take notes so that I can write some remarks for the councilman to use in response to the address. The councilman makes these evenings as pleasant as possible; we meet in a comfortable room with a big TV and order in dinner. We have to be focused on what we're doing, but we're still pretty relaxed, and there's a great feeling of camaraderie. For the most part, the councilman that I work for is understanding about other commitments in his employee's lives, as long as we're committed to doing our jobs well.

Because I'm on the staff of an elected official, I'm considered a government employee. That means I have good benefits, like excellent medical coverage. I also get to take advantage of some unofficial benefits. For example, I've eaten with my boss at some of the top restaurants and have gotten to know the *maître d's*. I can usually get a table easily at these restaurants and impress a date!

Resources

With the Internet and all the resources available at your school, you should be able to find information that helps you decide on a major, succeed in school, plan for and get a job, or go on to graduate school. This appendix lists English-related resources for you to consider when planning your college and career years.

Honor Societies

One way to network is to participate in English-related clubs or organizations, such as Sigma Tau Delta, the international English Honor Society. Through membership in this society, you may find a mentor, seek job advice, find a job, access information about contests or scholarships, submit your work for publication, be recognized for your work, or participate in and present professional work at conferences. You can also find internship and graduate assistantship opportunities available for members, and you receive the publications of the organization.

Sigma Tau Delta has over 600 active chapters, includes more than 900 faculty sponsors, and inducts approximately 7,000 members annually. You should check your particular school to see whether it has a chapter. And if so, determine how you might become a member and the cost of membership (this varies). (You might be automatically nominated based on your grades.) In this case, all you have to do is accept the membership. If you aren't asked, you can still pursue membership. Check with your local chapter about criteria for acceptance. Usually, you must have a minimum of a B or equivalent average in English and an overall class rank in the 35th per centile in general scholarship. You also must hav e completed at least thr ee semesters or fiv e quar ters of full-time college couses.

Sigma Tau Delta
Department of English
Northern Illinois University
DeKalb, IL 60115-2863
Phone: 815-753-1612
E-mail: sigmatd@niu.edu
Web site: www.english.org

Organizations, Associations, and Societies

In addition to E nglish honor societies, y ou'll find many mor e profes-sional and community organizations, associations, and societies. S ome of the most popular are included in this section. Keep in mind that this appendix, although covering the most important and common resources, only pr ovides a glimpse at the many differ ent organizations, associa-tions, and resources you can find within the field of E nglish. Look for other organizations during your studies or readings. Also, if you're look-ing for a par ticular organization or club, search for it using one of the Internet's many search tools.

AMERICAN COPY EDITORS SOCIETY (ACES)

If you plan to pursue a car eer in copy editing or ar e a copy editor, you may want to join the American Copy Editors Society (ACES). Founded in 1997, this pr ofessional journalism organization aims to pr ovide guidance, training, ne ws, and job oppor tunities for copy editors. The society is mostly geared toward newspaper copy editors, but other types of copy editors, as w ell as students, ar e welcomed, too. As a member, you receive a ne wsletter, a dir ectory of members, access to discussion boards, and reduced conference fees for certain conferences.

American Copy Editors Society
Web site: www.copydesk.org

American Society of Journalists and Authors

The American Society of Journalists and Authors (ASJA), the nation's leading organization of nonfiction pr ofessional freelance writers, helps freelance writers adv ance their writing car eers. As a member , you can get advice on ho w much to charge for wor k, check out fr eelance contracts, network with the 1,000+ other members, and par ticipate in the annual writer's conference.

> **American Society of Journalists and Authors**
> 1501 Broadway, Suite 302
> New York, NY 10036
> Phone : 212-997-0947
> Fax: 212-768-7414
> Web site: www.asja.org

Association for Women in Communications

If you are a woman and plan to wor k in some communication-r elated field (print and br oadcast journalism, television and radio pr oduction, film, adv ertising, public r elations, mar keting, graphic design, multimedia design, and photography), consider joining the Association for Women in Communications. Like other pr ofessional associations, the AWC pr ovides oppor tunities to networ k with other women in y our field, participate in conferences and meetings, and get job advice.

> **Association of Women in Communication**
> 780 Ritchie Hwy., Suite 28-S
> Severna Park, MD 21146
> Phone: 410-544-7442
> Fax: 410-544-4640
> Web site: www.womcom.org

Association of American Publishers

The principal association for the book publishing industr   y is the Association of American P ublishers (AAP), and as such, it r epresents publishers of all siz es and types located thr oughout the U nited States, including those that publish books, journals, computer softwar   e, audiovisual materials, databases, and interactiv   e and training CDs.

Even though you aren't likely to be a member , you can still access the Web site to get information on v arious publishers, as w ell as information on trends and news within the publishing field.

Association of American Publishers
71 Fifth Ave., 2nd Floor
New York, NY 10003
Phone: 212-255-0200
Fax: 212-255-7007
Web site: www.publishers.org

ASSOCIATION OF AUTHORS & PUBLISHERS

As a nonprofit association, the Authors & Publishers Association (APA) welcomes as members anyone associated with the production, development, marketing, or distribution of books. This includes authors (and would-be authors), editors, designers, ar tists, printers, publishers, self-publishers, mar keters, distributors, booksellers, and I   nternet pr ofessionals. The AP A publishes a ne wsletter and also maintains a talent pool or registry of members. What can you expect to find as a member? Current information and educational oppor tunities. I f you decide to write a book, you can find information, r esources, and industry representatives needed to produce and market your books.

Authors & Publishers Association
6124 Hwy. 6 N., PMB 109
Houston, TX 77084
Phone: 281-265-7342
E-mail: info@authorsandpublishers.org
Web site: www.authorsandpublishers.org

INVESTIGATIVE REPORTERS AND EDITORS

Founded in 1975, the I nvestigative R eporters and E ditors (IRE) is a forum for journalists from all over to share story ideas, news sources and contacts, and other information. I t seeks to pr omote high professional standards, provides opportunities for additional learning, and pr otects the rights of inv estigative journalists. I n addition to the networ king opportunities, members also receive a subscription to *The IRE Journal,* access to the IRE Resource Center (which contains an archive of 20,000+ investigative news stories, plus other databases and tip sheets), and invitations to member-only conferences, seminars, and workshops.

Investigative Reporters and Editors, Inc.
National Institute for Computer-Assisted Reporting, Inc.
138 Neff Annex
Missouri School of Journalism
Columbia, MO 65211
Phone: 573-882-2042
Fax: 573-882-5431
E-mail: info@ire.org
Web site: www.ire.org

MAGAZINE PUBLISHERS OF AMERICA

Magazine Publishers of America (MP A), the industr y association for consumer magazines, r epresents more than 240 U.S. publishing companies, as w ell as 80+ international companies. The Web site lists the following as their objectives:

◆ To support and promote the editorial and economic vitality and integrity of MPA member publications

◆ To advocate and litigate on behalf of the industry

◆ To defend the fr eedom to write and publish under the F irst Amendment

◆ To be the mar keting force to incr ease the shar e that magazines capture of advertising dollars and of reader time and money

◆ To be the primar y source of information and exper tise about the publishing industr y for both its members and the community at large

Magazine Publishers of America
810 Seventh Ave., 24th Floor
New York, NY 10019
Phone: 212-872-3700
Web site: www.magazine.org

MODERN LANGUAGE ASSOCIATION (MLA)

If you plan to teach E nglish, you'll find that the M odern Language Association (ML A) pr ovides r elevant oppor tunities and information. Founded in 1883, the Modern Language Association of America hosts an annual confer ence as w ell as local meetings. The association publishes the *MLA International Bibliography* (the only comprehensive bibliography in language and literatur e, av ailable in print, online, and CD-ROM versions), as w ell as sev eral major periodicals, a ne wsletter, and the *MLA Handbook for Writers of Research Papers*. In addition to its print resources, the ML A maintains a Web site and hosts some 130+ discussion groups that specialize in scholarly and teaching pursuits. You also can networ k with the some 30,000 members fr om 100 countries, sharing advice, research, teaching ideas, and more.

Membership is open to any one, including students, with an academic or professional interest in the fields of modern languages and literature. To be a member, you pay annual dues. Check the Web site for specific information on the costs of membership.

MLA
26 Broadway, 3rd Floor
New York, NY 10004-1789
Phone: 646-576-5000
Fax: 646-458-0030
Web site: www.mla.org

NATIONAL WRITERS UNION

If you plan to pursue a car eer as a fr eelance writer, you may consider joining the N ational Writers U nion. Like other unions, this writing-based group helps represent freelance writers in all genres, formats, and media. They list the follo wing as benefits of membership: help handling grievances, contract advice, a job hotline, health and professional liability insurance, lobbying efforts to protect the rights of writers, and much more. The union has r oughly 5,000 members, based in 17 local chapters. Check y our ar ea to see whether y ou have a local chapter . If not, you can still join the national gr oup. For more information, consult the union's Web site.

National Office of the National Writers Union
113 University Place, 6th Floor
New York, NY 10003
Phone: 212-254-0279
Fax: 212-254-0673
Web site: www.nwu.org

PUBLIC RELATIONS SOCIETY OF AMERICA

With its nearly 20,000 members and 114 chapters, the Public Relations Society of America (PRSA) is the world's largest organization for public relations pr ofessionals. As a member , y ou can networ k with other members, pursue additional pr ofessional dev elopment oppor tunities, and share information, r esearch, and advice. The PRSA has members from a wide v ariety of public r elations fields, including business and industry, technology, counseling firms, go vernment, associations, hospitals, schools, professional services firms, and nonprofit organizations.

PRSA
33 Maiden Ln., 11th Floor
New York, NY 10038-5150
Phone: 212-460-1400
Fax: 212-995-0757
Web site: www.prsa.org

SMALL PUBLISHERS, ARTISTS & WRITERS NETWORK

Small Publishers, Artists & Writers Network (SPAWN) is an organization designed for authors, illustrators, graphic designers, photographers, editors, self-publishers, and others inv olved in the pr ocess of publishing—helping them connect with each other and share information and ideas. In addition to facilitating an ex change of ideas, the site includes useful links to r esearch sour ces, publishers, printers, and the media.

SPAWN
PMB 123
323 E. Matilija St., Suite 110
Ojai, CA 93023

Phone: 818-886-4281
Fax: 818-886-3320
Web site: www.spawn.org

SOCIETY FOR TECHNICAL COMMUNICATION

The Society for Technical Communication (ST C), with some 18,000 members, seeks to adv ance the ar ts and sciences of technical communication. Among its members, you'll find technical writers and editors, content dev elopers, documentation specialists, technical illustrators, instructional designers, academics, information ar   chitects, usability professionals, visual designers,   Web designers and dev   elopers, and translators. If you plan to pursue any of these careers, you may want to join STC.

Society for Technical Communication
815 Fifteenth St. NW
Washington, DC 2005
Web site: www.stc.org

School and Career Web Sites

You can find a w ealth of job-related sites, some popular for all car eers, some dedicated to a par ticular type of car eer. This is just a shor t list; try searching for y our career of inter est and adding "jobs" to see what resources are available.

- ◆ **Advertising Job Bank:** Pwr.com/adjobbank
- ◆ **Advertising and Media Jobs Page:** www.nationjob.com/media
- ◆ **Careerbuilder.com:** www.careerbuilder.com
- ◆ **College Grad Job Hunter:** www.collegegrad.com
- ◆ **Graduate Guide (US Directory of Doctoral and Master's Programs):** www.graduateguide.com
- ◆ **Job Links for Journalists:** www.newslink.org/joblink.html
- ◆ **Marketing, Sales, and Advertising Jobs:** www.marketingjobs.com

- ◆ **Media Job Listings:** www.tvandradiojobs.com
- ◆ **Monster.com:** www.monster.com
- ◆ **Nonprofit Career Network:** www.nonprofitcareer.com
- ◆ **Opportunity Knocks:** www.OppportunityNOCS.org
- ◆ **The Write Jobs:** www.writerswrite.com/jobs

Journals, Magazines, Books, and More

Many organizations and associations publish journals. F or example, you may choose to subscribe to *Publishers Weekly* (www.publishers weekly.com), a magazine devoted to the publishing industry. It's expensive, but after a fe w weeks of r eading, you'll know the scoop on ev ery major (and even minor) publisher. In addition, you can find other publications helpful for your career and college studies. You can also find a wealth of books on the topics of English, on English majors, choosing a college, getting into graduate school, and finding a job (cr eating the perfect résumé, handling the interview, finding jobs online, and more). This section lists just a few key books.

Remember to check y our college's E nglish depar tment as w ell as your car eer center; they often hav e subscriptions to these journals. Career and job advice books ar e often housed in the car eer center library. Don't neglect the univ ersity library, either; it's likely to hav e a wealth of resources.

- ◆ **Career Opportunities in Advertising and Public Relations** by Shelly Field, F acts on F ile, J une 1997. Co vers pr ofiles of mor e than 80 different advertising and public relations jobs.

- ◆ **Careers for Bookworms & Other Literary Types, 3rd Edition,** by Marjorie Eberts and Margaret Gisler, McGraw-Hill, September 2002. A guide to careers for booklovers, including careers in book publishing, magazine writing, libraries, and more.

- ◆ **Graduate Programs in Humanities 2004** by Peterson's Guides, Peterson's, May 2003. A guide to U.S. graduate and pr ofessional programs. Co vers literatur e, histor y, philosophy , and r eligious studies.

- ◆ **Great Jobs for English Majors, 2nd Edition,** by Julie DeGalen and Stephen Lambert, McGraw-Hill, May 2000. From a series of books, this one focuses on careers specifically for English majors.

- ◆ **Great Jobs for Liberal Arts Majors** by B lythe Camenson, McGraw-Hill, April 1997. A series of books that explores employment opportunities and career paths.

- ◆ **Occupational Outlook Handbook: 2004–2005** by U.S. Department of Labor , J ist P ublishing, M ay 2004. ISBN: 1563709880. A go vernment publication that pr ovides job outlooks for many, many careers.

- ◆ **Opportunities in Publishing Careers, Revised Edition,** by Robert A. Carter and S. William Pattis, McGraw-Hill, September 2000. Another series of books that co vers compr ehensively a range of pr ofessions. I ncludes training and education r equirements and salary information.

- ◆ **Top Careers for Communications Graduates** by F erguson, Checkmark Books, November 2003. A guide to a wide variety of communication-related careers.

Self-Administered Aptitude Tests

With the wealth of information available on the Internet, you can find not only all kinds of career advice, but also assessment tests that ev aluate your type of personality, your particular skills and talents, and your other qualities. Keep in mind that these tests are based on your answers to the questions. I f you answer how you think you *should* answer, the results aren't going to be v alid. Answer honestly. Also, these tests giv e general advice and descriptions; there is no way to determine what type of person you are based on an online assessment. S till, assessment tests can give you some insight into your interests and abilities.

Keep in mind that some tests are provided for free. Some provide a minireview based on y our r esponses, and y ou can pay for a mor e detailed analysis. And some charge a fee to even take the test. Whether it costs money and how much money are not necessarily the best ways to ev aluate the effectiv eness of the test. I nstead, r ead about the test. What research is it based on? Who developed the test? What is the scientific theor y behind the testing? R eading this information will allo w you to better assess the test.

Also, taking the test can be fun (and addicting!). E veryone likes to know more about him- or herself. Explore the available testing and use it as one aspect in y our making y our decision, along with other information. Keep in mind, too, that aptitude tests can help with not only choosing a major but also finding a career suitable to your personality.

Most popular career tests include:

- Birkman Method
- Campbell Interest and Skill Survey (CISS)
- The Enneagram
- Kiersey Temperament Sorter
- The Kolbe Assessment
- Myers-Briggs Type Indicator (MBTI)
- Strong Interest Inventory (SII)
- System for Interactive Guidance and Information (SIGI)

The following sections describe some popular test and testing sites.

THE PRINCETON REVIEW CAREER QUIZ

Offered by The Princeton Review, a successful test-prep company, you can visit the company's Web site (www.princetonreview.com) and take its career tests.

JOHN HOLLAND'S SDS (SELF-DIRECTED SEARCH) — RIASEC

Available at www.self-directed-search.com, this test is taken online and costs under $10. D evised b y D r. J ohn H olland, it classifies y our answers among six personality traits (R ealistic, I nvestigative, Ar tistic, Social, Enterprising, and Conv entional) and assigns y ou a thr ee-letter "Holland code," representing the three traits, in order of relevance, that best describe you. An Interpretive Report then lists car eers that might interest y ou, each with fur ther information on such things as the amount of training needed. Similar lists of studies and leisure activities are also in the r eport. The report even offers lists for other combinations of the thr ee letters in y our code, just in case y ou're curious. The report ends with a list of resources for further information.

Career Interests Game

The Car eer I nterests G ame was designed b y D r. H olland's friend Richard Bolles (author of *What Color Is Your Parachute?*) as a briefer alternative to the RIASEC SDS. It appears in newer editions of Bolles' books and is also on the U niversity of M issouri Web site at http:// career.missouri.edu, where there is a link to the game. It's free of charge, so it may be a good way to sample H olland's method before deciding whether to pay for the original in-depth test and report.

Motivational Appraisal of Personal Potential (MAPP)

This test asks multiple-choice questions with thr ee possible answ ers that you rank in or der of y our preferences. The results of the tests ar e e-mailed to you. This test has been widely used not only by individuals but also by employers, who may use it to determine an applicant's suitability for a job, and by schools and teachers, who may use it to provide better guidance for students. The test can be found at www.assessment. com. Be warned that the pricing is not r eadily apparent until you have already "signed on" with your personal information.

Myers-Briggs Inventory

A test of personality type, its results can be applied to relationships and personal gr owth as w ell as y our car eer. It is av ailable thr ough sev eral Web sites. Some sites offer the test for free; some provide a quick summary but charge you for a full, in-depth assessment. Some charge a fee just to take the test. At the time of this writing, you could get some free assessments at www .humanmetrics.com as w ell as at haleonline.com. But because these sites change often, the pricing changes, and sites offering the tests come and go, y ou might do best by searching to find sites that offer tests (fr ee or other wise). U se a sear ch engine to find other sites that provide Myers-Briggs tests.

KEIRSEY CHARACTER SORTER

This test takes your answers and then decides which of the four tempera-ments best matches your personality (the idea is similar to Enneagram). You can take a sample test and get mor e information (including order-ing books dev oted to this test and its personality theor y) b y visiting www.keirsey.com.

TICKLE.COM

You can find a w ealth of useful as w ell as frivolous tests at Tickle.com. You can, for example, determine which *Friends* character is most like you. Likewise, you can also determine what r ock star you are. In addi-tion to these fun tests, the site offers a w ealth of useful personality and career testing, including:

- ◆ Career Interest Inventory
- ◆ Career Personality Test
- ◆ Right Job, Wrong Job
- ◆ Corporate Culture Test
- ◆ The Confidence Test
- ◆ Social Networking Test

In most cases, the tests are free and come with a basic report of your results. You can get a mor e in-depth, personaliz ed report for r oughly $20 a r eport. You can also subscribe to the ser vice and take as many tests as y ou want, getting detailed r esults for all the tests y ou take. Experiment, but keep in mind that you don't need a detailed report for every category and test. (After you get started, it's hard to stop, because you want to know more!)

Career Counseling

Although colleges and univ ersities hav e their o wn car eer counseling services, you may prefer an independent service, especially if you're not currently spending time on campus (for example, during the summer). These services may include subjects not offered at a small or specialized school, although plenty of on-campus ser vices do offer these things. Just remember that because these are commercial services, they will cost you something.

The best way to find car eer counseling in y our area is to ask others for recommendations. If you can't find someone from a recommenda-tion, look thr ough y our local paper (a neighborhood paper , if one is available). You might also look thr ough the Yellow Pages or search on the Internet. If you find some counselors thr ough your own research, call and talk with that person.   What ser vices does he or she pr ovide? What are the fees? What is the backgr ound of the counselor? D oes he or she specialize in any particular areas? Also, ask for references (and call and check them).

Index